CALLED TO COMMITMENT

CALLED TO COMMITMENT

Watchman Nee

Compiled by
JUDITH COUCHMAN

SERVANT PUBLICATIONS
ANN ARBOR, MICHIGAN

Vine Books is an imprint of Servant Publications especially designed to serve
evangelical Christians.

Compiled by Judith Couchman.

Published by Servant Publications
P.O. Box 8617
Ann Arbor, Michigan 48107

Cover design: Alan Furst, Minneapolis, Minnesota

99 00 01 02   10 9 8 7 6 5 4 3 2 1

Printed in the United States of America
ISBN 1-56955-094-8

LIBRARY OF CONGRESS CATALOGING-IN-PUBLICATION DATA

Nee, Watchman.
Called to commitment / Watchman Nee ; compiled by Judith Couchman.
    p.   cm.   —   (Life messages of great Christians)
ISBN 1-56955-094-8 (alk. paper)
1. Devotional calendars. 2. Spiritual life—Christianity Meditations.   I.
Couchman, Judith, 1953-   . II. Title.   III. Series.
BV4811.N44   1999
242'.2—dc21   99-30462
                                                      CIP

For Mary Brosa,
a loving and committed friend

CONTENTS

ACKNOWLEDGMENTS

Many thanks to the team at Servant Publications for supporting this book and the *Life Messages of Great Christians* series, especially Bert Ghezzi. I'm also grateful to editor Liz Heaney and copy editor Deena Davis for their contributions to this book, and to my Vision Group friend Lisa Marzano, who inputted text and wrote many of the thoughts, questions, and prayers.

All of us thank Herbert L. Fader and Christian Fellowship Publishers, Inc., Willard Stone and Christian Literature Crusade, and The Sure Foundation for granting the permission to reprint from Watchman Nee's books.

And once again I thank those who prayed for me and the compilation process: Charette Barta, Opal Couchman, Win Couchman, Madalene Harris, Karen Hilt, Shirley Honeywell, and Nancy Lemons.

*Today I would like to say to my younger fellow work-
ers: If you are unable to stand the grinding of the
Cross, you are useless in the Lord's hand. Only the spirit of the Lamb, gentle and meek, is approved of the
Lord. Your ambition and ability are useless to Him....
In the Church, bearing the cross, not reasoning, is the
law.* [1]

Watchman Nee, a Chinese evangelist and church planter, offered this advice to spiritual workers in his home-land. These were hard words to some, but to Nee they were liberating. He believed that Christians are called to commit-ment, and the way of the Cross is the path to inner freedom and usefulness to God.

This was also hard-won advice, for most of Nee's life was characterized by the "grinding of the cross" and surrendering all to his beloved Christ. He did not preach what he had not lived.

Born in Swatow, China, in 1903, Nee was the answer to his mother's prayers for a son. Growing up he learned about Christ and salvation, but as a young man he mocked anything "Christian." However, when Nee's mother was born again she changed so dramatically that he decided Christianity was more than a mere creed. At age seventeen he accepted Christ, rec-ognizing the true scope of his decision.

"I felt that if I should accept Jesus to be my Savior, I must at the same time receive Him as my Lord; I would have to serve Him throughout my whole life," he explained. "Accordingly, my receiving the Lord's salvation must be twofold: I must not only be saved from my sins, I must also be saved from the world. I was convinced that I could not set aside the Lord's calling, merely becoming a saved person and not a serving one as well." [2] Nee was so earnest about his commitment, for the next two years he confessed his sins and apologized to "at least two to three hundred people,"[3] to be sure no obstacles stood between the Holy Spirit and him.

Despite Nee's barrier-free approach to God, his life was filled with other obstacles that challenged and refined his faith. He experienced serious illnesses, expulsions from fellowships to whom he ministered, persecution from relatives, times of working in obscurity, and misunderstandings from friends. None of these deterred him from proclaiming Christ, desiring a deeper walk with Him, and helping believers grow in their faith. Under his ministry revival broke out, churches sprang up, and the Chinese church grew remarkably.

Even when the Communist regime captured China, Nee would not relinquish his commitment, and consequently he spent the last twenty years of his life in prison. "Do not worry," he wrote to his sister-in-law, "because I maintain my joy [in Christ]."[4] A year before his own death alone in a labor camp, he grieved the death of his wife, Charity.

Nee's last written words, tucked under the mattress near his pillow, read: *Christ is the Son of God, who died to atone for men's sins and who rose on the third day. This is the greatest fact in the universe. I believe in Christ and die. Signed, Watchman Nee.* The great teacher died as he had lived.

Thankfully, Nee's works didn't die with him. Today at least forty books, based on his sermons and teachings, are in print and still exhort and encourage Christians around the world. God has fulfilled his servant's desire, expressed in the last stanzas of a poem he wrote as a young man:

In this time of trial, O Lord, I pray
That you'll wipe all my hidden tears away;
Let me learn, O Lord, You are my reward,
Let me be others' blessing all my days. [5]

1. *The Finest of the Wheat, Volume 1* (New York: Christian Fellowship Publishers, 1992), 14.
2. Wheat, 4.
3. Wheat, 9.
4. Wheat, 41.
5. Wheat, 1.

PART ONE

Faith and Commitment

Jesus, I my cross have taken,
All to leave and follow Thee;
Destitute, despised, forsaken,
Thou from hence my all shall be.
Perish every fond ambition,
All I've sought, and hoped and known;
Yet how rich is my condition.
God and heav'n are still my own!

"JESUS, I MY CROSS HAVE TAKEN"
BY HENRY F. LYTE

WATCHMAN NEE'S INSIGHT
Christ calls us to total commitment to Him.

Peace With God

THOUGHT FOR TODAY

God wants us to be reconciled to Him.

WISDOM FROM SCRIPTURE

Therefore, since we have been justified through faith, we have peace with God through our Lord Jesus Christ, through whom we have gained access by faith into this grace in which we now stand. And we rejoice in the hope of the glory of God.

Not only so, but we also rejoice in our sufferings, because we know that suffering produces perseverance; perseverance, character; and character, hope.

And hope does not disappoint us, because God has poured out his love into our hearts by the Holy Spirit, whom he has given us.

You see, at just the right time, when we were still powerless, Christ died for the ungodly.

Very rarely will anyone die for a righteous man, though for a good man someone might possibly dare to die.

But God demonstrates his own love for us in this: While we were still sinners, Christ died for us.

Since we have now been justified by his blood, how much more shall we be saved from God's wrath through him!

For if, when we were God's enemies, we were reconciled to him through the death of his Son, how much more, having been reconciled, shall we be saved through his life!

ROMANS 5:1-10, NIV

Have you been reconciled to God? Are you a saved person? Have you made peace with God through the Lord Jesus? The divine way of reconciliation is that "we have peace with God through our Lord Jesus Christ"—that we are "reconciled to him through the death of his Son" (Rom 5:1, 10a).

You do not make peace with God through your so-called good works. For although you may already be a church member—having been baptized and having received the Lord's Supper—or have often attended church worship and frequently read the Bible and prayed, or have even sometimes asked people to believe in the Lord or have preached and led in the church, you are still a lost sinner and an enemy to God. You need to be reconciled to Him through the death of the Lord Jesus by believing that Christ died, bore your sins and accomplished the work of redemption for you.

Do not conceive the idea that your good works and zeal will reconcile you to God. If God views the death of the Lord Jesus to be absolutely necessary, then anything short of His death is totally unacceptable. Men will either be reconciled through Jesus Christ or continue to be enemies of His by trusting in their own works.

God has paid all the cost for reconciliation. He has already accomplished the work of perfect redemption. The Lord Jesus has achieved everlasting salvation. Whether to be saved or lost is now the question which is put before you. You cannot be saved by your own righteousness, yet neither must you perish because of your sins. Whether you are saved or lost depends upon your willingness to accept the salvation the Lord Jesus has accomplished for you.

During the American Civil War a victorious general issued an order to his defeated foes which went something like this: "I now set apart several miles of land as a refuge of peace. All who lay down their arms and pass over into this parcel of land shall be saved; all others will be killed without mercy." Many believed the order. They laid down their arms and entered the designated area. These were all saved. But some were doubtful and refused to enter the land of refuge; with the result that they were all eventually killed.

God has designed Calvary's cross to be the land of peace for all men. You, like so many in this world, have been at enmity with Him; yet if at this moment you are willing to lay aside your sins and stand at the foot of the cross, trusting in the peace which Christ has achieved for you, you shall be saved. But if you still doubt and do not believe, you shall die in your sins. In the Civil War incident there was no difference between those who lived and those who died except as to whether they entered or did not enter the appointed area of land. Some might have moved to within a foot of the land, where they could easily enter in with but one step. Yet they were killed because they remained outside the land. Hence do not delay any longer. Do not be lost for lacking only one brief step. Trust in the Lord and you shall be saved. "Whosoever will, let him take the water of life freely" (Rev 22:17d). Why not do it today?

Now if you are truly willing to accept the peace which the Lord has achieved, you will be delivered from both your sins and their penalty. For the Bible declares that "God was in Christ reconciling the world unto himself, not imputing their trespasses unto them" (2 Cor 5:19a, b). Moreover, what joy we experience when we are no longer under condemnation!— "We also rejoice in God through our Lord Jesus Christ, by whom we have now received the reconciliation" (Rom 5:11).

I would ask one final time, Have you been reconciled to God? You should answer quickly. Your future depends on your answer today. "Now, then, we are ambassadors for Christ, as though God did beseech you by us; we pray you in Christ's stead, be ye reconciled to God" (2 Cor 5:20). "He came and preached peace to you who were afar off [the gentiles], and to them that were nigh [the Jews]" (Eph 2:17). May the Holy Spirit touch the heart of anyone who receives the message, causing him to accept Jesus as Lord and Savior.

"O Lord, I was Your enemy, but now I am willing to believe You because of the love You manifested on the Cross and because of the peace which You have achieved. O Lord, save me, a sinner!"

—Full of Grace and Truth

QUESTIONS TO CONSIDER
1. Have you been reconciled to God?
2. If so, how do you know this is true?

A PRAYERFUL RESPONSE
Lord, thank You for Your gift of reconciliation. Amen.

Saved and Assured by Grace

THOUGHT FOR TODAY

God's Word is true regardless of our feelings.

WISDOM FROM SCRIPTURE

As for you, you were dead in your transgressions and sins, in which you used to live when you followed the ways of this world and of the ruler of the kingdom of the air, the spirit who is now at work in those who are disobedient.

All of us also lived among them at one time, gratifying the cravings of our sinful nature and following its desires and thoughts. Like the rest, we were by nature objects of wrath.

But because of his great love for us, God, who is rich in mercy, made us alive with Christ even when we were dead in transgressions—it is by grace you have been saved.

And God raised us up with Christ and seated us with him in the heavenly realms in Christ Jesus, in order that in the coming ages he might show the incomparable riches of his grace, expressed in his kindness to us in Christ Jesus.

For it is by grace you have been saved, through faith—and this not from yourselves, it is the gift of God—not by works, so that no one can boast.

EPHESIANS 2:1-9, NIV

INSIGHTS FROM WATCHMAN NEE

Since the Bible states that we who believe in the Lord are saved, we therefore are saved people. Regardless whether we feel saved or not, we are saved if God says so. You have already trusted in the Lord Jesus and your sins are already washed by His precious blood; consequently, you are already saved. Why? Because this is what the Word of God makes clear.

Suppose, for example, there is a poor family which is suffering great privation through financial difficulties. The head of the family writes to his well-to-do friend, asking for help. Several days pass and no reply comes. He begins to think that his friend probably despises him and refuses to help. He feels depressed in his heart. The more he ponders the situation, the more he feels his friend will not help him. He then begins to share his thought with his neighbors. Some neighbors say that true friendship includes sharing the wealth, and that therefore his friend has no reason to refuse to help. When this head of the household hears hopeful words, he feels happy; but when he hears disappointing words, he is dejected.

Yet one day a letter arrives at his home from his friend. His heart beats quickly, not knowing whether there would be a promise of help. Upon opening the letter, he shouts to his family members: "Now at last everything is settled. He wrote me with his own hand that hereafter he will be responsible for all our needs. I do not care what people say, whether expressing hopefulness or hopelessness, for *he himself* says he will take the responsibility. We can now live in peace."

Are not many believers like this poor man before the letter arrived? They vacillate from one feeling to another as they listen to people's opinions. But just as this poor man finally came to rest in the word of his friend, so our hearts should be firmly established in the Word of God. God declares that if we believe in Jesus Christ, we have obtained our salvation. And His having said it should settle everything. Hence can there be any room for doubting? Does it matter how we feel? Or how other people think? God says we are saved, and that should be enough. His word is that final judgment. Since God has generously declared His truth, let us accept His word in faith without doubting.

Yet some will insist on saying this: "What has been mentioned already is indeed true, but I am afraid my faith is not perfect, and therefore, I am not saved."

The Bible only knows the difference between "believe" and "not believe"—and it knows nothing about so-called imperfect faith. We ought to be very clear in our understanding that there is no merit in our believing in the Lord Jesus. God does not save us because we have the merit of faith. Believing is receiving (see Jn 1:12). John 3:16 says God "gave" the Lord Jesus to us and John 1:12 says we "receive" Him. That is all. One giving and one receiving. There is no merit accrued to the sinner on any account. For salvation is all accomplished by the Lord Jesus.

Who among us is not a sinner? We were all dead in trespasses and sins. How truly pitiful! But the Holy Spirit comes to convict us of sin. How terrible is the penalty of sin! Who will not tremble at the thought of the future? What is even more tragic is that we have no way to save ourselves. Sinking in sin's mire and being unable to extricate ourselves is really a frightening experience. Yet thanks and praise be to the Lamb who was slain! He came and died on the cross for us. He stood in the place of sinners. He loved us and gave Himself up for us. He became our salvation. When He died, He cried, "It is finished" (Jn 19:30). How lovely He is! O Lord, we are eternally grateful to You for Your immense grace! To believe in the

Lord Jesus means nothing else than that we are hopeless and helpless sinners and willing to be saved by Him. He comes to save, and we want to be saved. That is all. Here there is not even the slightest consideration of perfect or imperfect faith.

Has not the Lord Jesus Himself said that he "that cometh to me I will in no wise cast out" (Jn 6:37)? Praise God, Christ is truthful and trustworthy here. With Him there is no guile or guile in His Word. When He declares He will never cast out those who come to Him, He means it. He will save all who know their sins and are willing to accept Him as Savior. "Come unto me, all ye that labor and are heavy laden, and I will give you rest" (Mt 11:28). "If any man thirst, let him come unto me and drink" (Jn 7:37). This is the Lord's standing invitation.

It is not really faith that saves us. It is His grace and faithfulness. God loves to save us, and He is gracious to us. Why do we not believe? Is there any good reason to doubt? The compassions of Christ ought to fill our hearts and displace all wondering, uncertain thoughts.

—Full of Grace and Truth

QUESTIONS TO CONSIDER

1. Do you feel assured of your salvation? Why, or why not?
2. How can you know that Christ is "truthful and trustworthy" about your salvation?

A PRAYERFUL RESPONSE

Lord, I will trust in the surety of Your salvation. Amen.

DAY 3

Clothed With Christ

THOUGHT FOR TODAY

Christ is our righteousness.

WISDOM FROM SCRIPTURE

For Christ's love compels us, because we are convinced that one died for all, and therefore all died.

And he died for all, that those who live should no longer live for themselves but for him who died for them and was raised again.

So from now on we regard no one from a worldly point of view. Though we once regarded Christ in this way, we do so no longer.

Therefore, if anyone is in Christ, he is a new creation; the old has gone, the new has come!

All this is from God, who reconciled us to himself through Christ and gave us the ministry of reconciliation: that God was reconciling the world to himself in Christ, not counting men's sins against them. And he has committed to us the message of reconciliation.

We are therefore Christ's ambassadors, as though God were making his appeal through us. We implore you on Christ's behalf: Be reconciled to God.

God made him who had no sin to be sin for us, so that in him we might become the righteousness of God.

2 CORINTHIANS 5:14-21, NIV

If our righteousness before God were our conduct we would be very unstable, because our conduct is sometimes good and sometimes bad. Furthermore, our good conduct is always limited, and can never meet the standard of God. Thank God, the righteousness we have before Him is not our conduct, but Christ; we are therefore immovable before Him.

Today you may not be very strong and good. Satan will come and tempt you, saying, "What are you, after all? God will not have such a person as you." But you can reply: "You have forgotten, Satan, that my righteousness before God is not my good conduct of yesterday nor is it my less good conduct of today. My righteousness before Him is Christ. Christ has not changed today, so my righteousness remains unchanged."

Should the garment we wear be of our own making it would be dirty rags and we would be quite unable to meet God. But we are today clothed with Christ; hence we have boldness to see God. Oh! This is deliverance, this is emancipation, this is the foundation of Christian doctrine.

Suppose we imagine ourselves asking a brother who knows the Word of God: "Will your righteousness ever fail?" He will answer, "No, never." "But will your conduct ever fail?" we may ask. He will say, "Certainly." Do you see that his righteousness will never fail, though his conduct may? His righteousness is not his conduct. If this were true, then when his conduct failed, his righteousness would fail, too. Yet his righteousness is not his conduct; it is not that which is subject to failure. His righteousness is the Christ who never fails. And so our righteousness, too, never fails; it is as unfailing as Christ is. Now this may sound too bold, but it is the Word of God. Our righteousness is Christ.

Because He never fails, our righteousness never fails either.

Some may perhaps inquire, "Does it then mean that our bad conduct does not matter?" It definitely does matter. For the Bible shows us that a Christian has two garments: one is the Lord Jesus, for He is our robe, He is our righteousness. The other is the bright and pure fine linen of Revelation 19:8: "For the fine linen is the righteous acts of the saints." ("Righteous acts" is "righteousness" in the original, meaning the many acts of righteousness.) All the good conduct of a Christian—all his outward righteousness—comes from grace as a result of the working of the Holy Spirit in him; they are not something which he has naturally. As we approach God we are not naked, because we are clothed with Christ who is our righteousness, that which is called the righteousness of the saints (see 2 Cor 5:10; 1 Cor 4:5).

There is one name in the Old Testament which is very precious. It is "Jehovah our righteousness" (Jer 23:6; 33:16). Jehovah is our righteousness, therefore our righteousness is not our conduct. May God open our eyes that we may see the gospel, even the foundation of the gospel. As we come to God, Christ—not our conduct—is our righteousness. The Lord is our righteousness. We come to God through Christ. What else is as firm and immovable as this?

Each time we approach God, we need to remember that Christ is our righteousness. If we see Him as this, we will stand in the presence of God with confidence. We will come as little children, saying to Him, "Look, I come today clothed with Christ." God looks, and He finds no defect. The more He looks the better we look, for Christ is absolutely without blemish. He is perfect.

"His grace, through which he hath made us accepted in the Beloved" (Eph 1:6). This verse includes the thought of our being accepted in the Beloved. Just as God accepts His beloved Son, even so He accepts us in the Beloved. We are accepted in the Beloved, and we are as accepted as the Beloved. God accepts us as He accepts His own Son. Whatever position the beloved Son has, belongs to all who are in the Beloved. This is truly most glorious.

Losing boldness in coming to God is due to our looking at ourselves. Whenever we are afraid of seeing God, we have not seen Christ. If we see Him—and not ourselves—we shall have confidence every time we approach God. Praise Him, our righteousness is not susceptible to change. Should some ask us if the conduct of a Christian, his zeal and love, is open to change, our answer would have to be yes. We would be deceiving ourselves if we were to deny such a possibility. Yet if the subject were our righteousness, we would say it is not subject to change, for it is unchangeable. The Word of God clearly declares that the unchanging Christ is our righteousness.

"Of (God) are ye in Christ Jesus, who was made unto us ... righteousness" (1 Cor 1:30). After the Lord was raised from the dead and was made Christ, God put us in Him as our righteousness. We are clothed with Christ our righteousness. As Christ never changes before God, so we may come to Him daily with boldness.

—*The Glory of His Life*

QUESTIONS TO CONSIDER

1. Has the truth of "Christ, my righteousness" penetrated your heart and life?
2. What can help you comprehend your righteousness in Christ?

A PRAYERFUL RESPONSE

Lord, I boldly approach You through the righteousness of Christ. Amen.

Not of This World

THOUGHT FOR TODAY

Because of the cross, we are free from bondage.

WISDOM FROM SCRIPTURE

May I never boast of anything except the cross of our Lord Jesus Christ, by which the world has been crucified to me, and I to the world.

For if we have been united with him in a death like his, we will certainly be united with him in a resurrection like his.

We know that our old self was crucified with him so that the body of sin might be destroyed, and we might no longer be enslaved to sin.

For whoever has died is freed from sin.

But if we have died with Christ we believe that we will also live with him.

We know that Christ, being raised from the dead, will never die again; death no longer has dominion over him.

The death he died, he died to sin, once for all; but the life he lives, he lives to God.

So you also must consider yourselves dead to sin and alive to God in Christ Jesus.

GALATIANS 6:14; ROMANS 6:5-11, NRSV

INSIGHTS FROM WATCHMAN NEE

Our deliverance from the world begins, not with our giving up this or that but with our seeing, as with God's eyes, that it is a world under sentence of death as in the words, "Babylon the great is fallen, is fallen" (Rev 18:2). Now a sentence of death is always passed, not on the dead but on the living. And in one sense the world is a living force today, relentlessly pursuing and seeking out its subjects. But while it is true that when sentence is pronounced, death lies still in the future, it is nevertheless certain. A person under sentence of death has no future beyond the confines of a condemned cell. Likewise the world, being under sentence, has no future.

The world system has not yet been "wound up," as we say, and terminated by God, but the winding up is a settled matter. It makes all the difference to us that we *see* this. Some folk seek deliverance from the world in asceticism, and neither eat nor drink. As Christians we both eat and drink, but we do so in the realization that eating and drinking belong to the world and, with it, are under the death sentence, so they have no grip upon us.

At the end of his letter to the Galatians, Paul states this very clearly. "But God forbid that I should glory, save in the cross of our Lord Jesus Christ, by whom the world is crucified unto me, and I unto the world" (6:14). Have you noticed something striking about this verse? In relation to the world it speaks of the two aspects of the work of the cross already hinted at in our last chapter. "I have been crucified unto the world" is a statement which we find fairly easy to fit into our understanding of being crucified with Christ as defined in such passages as Romans 6. But here it specifically says, too, that "the world has been crucified to me."

When God comes to you and me with the revelation of the

finished work of Christ, He not only shows us ourselves there on the cross, He shows us our world there too. If you and I cannot escape the judgment of the cross, then neither can the world escape the judgment of the cross. Have I really seen this? That is the question. When I see it, then I do not try to repudiate a world I love; I see that the cross has repudiated it. I do not try to escape a world that clings to me; I see that by the cross I have escaped.

—*The Finest of the Wheat, Volume 2*

QUESTIONS TO CONSIDER

1. To you, what does it mean to be "dead to the world"?
2. How can you be "dead to the world" and still live in it?

A PRAYERFUL RESPONSE

Lord, thank You that through the cross I am free from the world. Amen.

DAY 5

Confessing the Lord

THOUGHT FOR TODAY

When we confess Christ as Lord, He will confess us before the Father.

WISDOM FROM SCRIPTURE

Brothers, my heart's desire and prayer to God for the Israelites is that they may be saved.

For I can testify about them that they are zealous for God, but their zeal is not based on knowledge.

Since they did not know the righteousness that comes from God and sought to establish their own, they did not submit to God's righteousness.

Christ is the end of the law so that there may be righteousness for everyone who believes.

Moses describes in this way the righteousness that is by the law: "The man who does these things will live by them."

But the righteousness that is by faith says: "Do not say in your heart, 'Who will ascend into heaven?'" (that is, to bring Christ down) "or 'Who will descend into the deep?'" (that is, to bring Christ up from the dead).

But what does it say? "The word is near you; it is in your mouth and in your heart," that is, the word of faith we are proclaiming:

That if you confess with your mouth, "Jesus is Lord," and believe in your heart that God raised him from the dead, you will be saved.

For it is with your heart that you believe and are justified, and it is with your mouth that you confess and are saved.

ROMANS 10:1-10, NIV

INSIGHTS FROM WATCHMAN NEE

Once a person has trusted in the Lord, he must confess the Lord before men. He should not hide his faith but should publicly confess it. The importance of such confession is both laid down in the Bible and is borne out by our experience.

Suppose a baby makes no sound after one, two, or even three years of age. What would you think? If the child never talks in childhood, most probably he will be dumb for the rest of his life. If he cannot call "Papa," and "Mama," as a child, he likely never will. Likewise, one who believes in the Lord must confess Him immediately, or else he may be dumb throughout his life.

Today we have seen too much of how people can be Christians for ten or twenty years and still be mute. Because they are inarticulate during the first and second week of their Christian life, they remain so ever after. The best opportunity to confess the Lord comes right at the beginning. If one starts immediately, the way of confession is forever open. So one must force oneself to speak out right after he believes in the Lord, even if he feels it difficult and finds himself rather unwilling. He should confess the Lord before his friends and relatives; otherwise he will be mute for life. We do not want to have any dumb believers; therefore let us learn to open our mouths at the very beginning. Go and find the opportunity to confess our Lord. Confession is a big thing for new believers and a very profitable thing, too. If it is not done at the onset, it will become almost impossible later on, unless by the special mercy of God there comes a revival to the soul.

"For with the heart man believeth unto righteousness; and with the mouth confession is made unto salvation" (Rom 10:10). The first half has to do with God while the second half has to do with men. No one can see whether you have believed or not; but if you come to God really believing, you will be justified before Him. Nevertheless, if you believe in your heart but never confess with your mouth, though justified before God, you will not be delivered from the world. The people of this world will not acknowledge you as a saved person. They will still reckon you as one of them, for they have not witnessed any difference between you and them. On this account the Bible emphatically states that besides believing with the heart there must also be confessing with the mouth.

I have seen some people who at first pretended to be Christians but finally turned out to be true Christians. At first they just feigned belief, but as they stood up to declare, "I have believed in Jesus," they became true believers! Many undecided ones, at the time they confess, seal their faith in the Lord. This is comparable to cement that originally is just an easily scattered powder; soon after it is mixed with water, though, it begins to congeal. Many workers have had the experience of seeing people's faith confirmed by saying, "I believe." In preaching the gospel, we help people by pushing, not by pulling. We encourage them to stand up and to confess, "I believe in the Lord Jesus." If anyone confesses with his mouth as well as believes with his heart, he becomes a separated person.

"Every one therefore who shall confess me before men, him will I also confess before my Father who is in heaven" (Mt 10:32). How we thank the Lord for His confessing us in the future if we confess Him today. Today, before men who are as the grass of the field, we confess Him as Jesus Christ, the Son of the Living God, but on that day when our Lord shall come back He will confess us before His Father and before His angels in glory. If we feel it difficult to confess Him today, will He find it hard to confess us in that day?

"But whosoever shall deny me before men, him will I also deny before my Father who is in heaven" (Mt 10:33). How great is the contrast! If we find it burdensome to confess before men that we have a Man who is above all men, a Man who is truly the Son of God, how will He confess us before His Father when He shall come with His angels in glory—we who are so ragged? This indeed is a serious matter. Please remember that in comparison to His confessing us one day, our confessing Him is not at all difficult. For Him to confess us is mystifying—for we are but prodigal sons coming home. We have absolutely nothing in ourselves. Let us, then, all the more ardently confess Him, since we know that He will confess us.

—*The Good Confession*

QUESTIONS TO CONSIDER
1. Have you publicly confessed Christ as Lord?
2. Has this affected your spiritual walk? If so, how?

A PRAYERFUL RESPONSE
Lord, I will find opportunities to confess You as Lord. Amen.

DAY 6

Living Faith

THOUGHT FOR TODAY

Faith and works belong together.

WISDOM FROM SCRIPTURE

In the same way, faith by itself, if it is not accompanied by action, is dead.

But someone will say, "You have faith; I have deeds." Show me your faith without deeds, and I will show you my faith by what I do.

You believe that there is one God. Good! Even the demons believe that—and shudder.

You foolish man, do you want evidence that faith without deeds is useless?

Was not our ancestor Abraham considered righteous for what he did when he offered his son Isaac on the altar?

You see that his faith and his actions were working together, and his faith was made complete by what he did.

And the scripture was fulfilled that says, "Abraham believed God, and it was credited to him as righteousness," and he was called God's friend.

You see that a person is justified by what he does and not by faith alone.

In the same way, was not even Rahab the prostitute considered righteous for what she did when she gave lodging to the spies and sent them off in a different direction?

As the body without the spirit is dead, so faith without deeds is dead.

JAMES 2:17-26, NIV

INSIGHTS FROM WATCHMAN NEE

God tested Abraham in order to see that his heart was toward Him and that his faith was real. God asked him to offer up on the altar his son Isaac, the one who was divinely appointed to be his heir—and there to be slain and burnt. Yet how would God's promise ever be fulfilled if Abraham loved God, and burned Isaac? If he wanted to fulfill God's promise he could not comply with God's request.

Far from being unified, these two factors seem contradictory to each other. Yet to a living faith they are unified and not contradictory. It is God who promises, and it is God who requires. God will never contradict Himself. Between promise and request God will open a new way, that is to say, the way of resurrection: "Accounting that God is able to raise up, even from the dead" (Heb 11:19).

Abraham's faith is thus defined: Even though I slay Isaac and offer him as a burnt-offering, I still believe Your promised words—"in Isaac shall thy seed be called"—will be fulfilled, for you shall raise up Isaac from the dead. So when he went off to the appointed place to offer up Isaac, he went with a determined heart. He actually bound Isaac and raised high his knife. His heart toward God was absolute, there being no reservation. His faith in God was firm, and void of doubt. And when the angel of the Lord called to him and said, "Lay not thy hand upon the lad, neither do thou any thing unto him" (Gn 22:12), he did also "in a figure" receive him back (see Heb

11:19). Abraham's offering up of his only begotten son was a work of faith. And this is called justification by works.

"Thou seest that faith wrought with his works, and by works was faith made perfect" (Jas 2:22). This continues on from the preceding thought. By offering up Isaac on the altar Abraham was justified by works and we come to realize that faith runs parallel with works. To phrase it another way, faith and works operate together. Abraham's work is performed through his faith, and faith is perfected by his works. A faith which has not been tested is undependable. By his offering Isaac, Abraham's faith is both proven and perfected.

"And the scripture was fulfilled which saith, 'And Abraham believed God, and it was reckoned unto him for righteousness; and he was called the friend of God' " (verse 23). "Abraham believed God, and it was reckoned unto him for righteousness"—this word is recorded in Genesis 15:6. What is the relationship between the offering up of Isaac in Genesis 22 to that word? Why would James quote it in his epistle when he suggests that the offering up of Isaac is a justification by works? And he even adds that the scripture was fulfilled.

The relationship is simply this: that justification by works fulfills justification by faith. It appears as though justification by faith is a prophecy and that justification by works is the fulfillment of that prophecy. He who has faith must have works, for works explain the reality of faith. Abraham believed in God, he was reckoned as righteous, and he was also called the friend of God. Hence Abraham's work in offering up Isaac is the fulfillment of Abraham's faith in God. In short, his offering up of Isaac demonstrates to us his faith in God.

"Ye see, then, that by works a man is justified, and not by

faith only" (verse 24). Since Genesis 22 is the fulfillment of Genesis 15, and since works are the expression of faith, because faith without works is dead and faith is made perfect by works, the more a man is justified by works and not only by faith. Let us note that James has not said that a man is justified by works and not by faith; he merely says that a man is justified by works and not only by faith. And by this he means to say that after a man is justified by faith he needs to prove and to be made perfect in that faith through justification by works, even as Abraham after he was justified by faith was tested by God and thus was justified by works.

"Likewise also was not Rahab the harlot justified by works, when she had received the messengers, and had sent them out another way?" (verse 25). James first cites an excellent person such as Abraham to show that he was not only justified by faith but also by works. Next, though, he cites a woman such as Rahab to show that she too was justified by works, for she received the messengers and sent them out another way.

What kind of work is this work? "By faith the harlot Rahab perished not with them that believed not, when she had received the spies with peace" (Heb 11:31). This work is also a work of faith. Faith and works are inseparable; they are the two sides of one thing. It is called *faith* in Hebrews and *works* in James. Works are the expressions of faith, whereas faith is the source of works. To say that there is faith and yet there be no works of faith shown, that faith is dead. Consequently, after there is a justification by faith, there must also be the justification by works.

"For as the body without the spirit is dead, so faith without works is dead also" (verse 26). There is a kind of faith which has no works, being nothing but a vain boast; and it is dead. But there is another kind of faith, and works make perfect the faith. James uses what Abraham and Rahab did as evidences to prove his point. And finally, he uses this other illustration: "As the body without the spirit is dead, so faith without works is dead."

—*Gospel Dialogue*

QUESTIONS TO CONSIDER

1. In your walk with Christ, do you see gaps between faith and action?
2. If so, what steps can you take to narrow this gap?

A PRAYERFUL RESPONSE

Lord, help me to express both faith and action. Amen.

Confessing Our Sins

THOUGHT FOR TODAY

Confession to God and man promotes spiritual growth.

WISDOM FROM SCRIPTURE

Blessed is he whose transgressions are forgiven, whose sins are covered.

Blessed is the man whose sin the Lord does not count against him and in whose spirit is no deceit.

When I kept silent, my bones wasted away through my groaning all day long.

For day and night your hand was heavy upon me; my strength was sapped as in the heat of summer.

Then I acknowledged my sin to you and did not cover up my iniquity. I said, "I will confess my transgressions to the Lord"—and you forgave the guilt of my sin.

Therefore let everyone who is godly pray to you while you may be found; surely when the mighty waters rise, they will not reach him.

You are my hiding place; you will protect me from trouble and surround me with songs of deliverance.

PSALM 32:1-7, NIV

INSIGHTS FROM WATCHMAN NEE

"He that covereth his sins shall not prosper; but whoso confesseth and forsaketh them shall have mercy" (Prv 28:13). Let us be those who confess their sins committed in the past. Let us apologize to men if we have sinned against them. Let us confess to God if we have offended Him. Otherwise we may suffer loss in the future.

Once when Evan Roberts was asked about spiritual growth, he answered, "When did you last confess your sin?" The one who heard this did not understand what was meant. He wondered how one would confess his sin as though it were a daily affair. Was it like taking meals every day? He recalled that he had not confessed his sins for many years. Subsequently, he came to know what Mr. Roberts had meant. He, too, began to see that a Christian makes progress as he confesses his sins. We must confess to God when God is offended and confess to men when man is offended; and this will thus enable us to grow in spiritual life.

How many feel sorrowful after they have sinned? If people do not feel sorrowful, this indicates they have failed in the matter of confessing sin. But if any Christian will clear up his sins against God and men with confession, he will proceed well in the course which is before him. He will walk farther than other Christians. How sad that many believers have too little sensitivity toward sin.

Many dare not sin for the sake of saving face, either for their own reputation or for the reputation of their family. Some dare not sin because they do not have the capital to sin (that is to say, they lack the ability or opportunity). Some others do not sin for fear of its consequence. But let me ask you, How many of you do not dare to sin because of its hatefulness, uncleanness, and opposition to God? I am surprised at finding people sleeping soundly and eating well after they have committed sins. Our God hates sin. I hate sin, not because of saving face or lack of capital or fear of its consequences, but because of God. In order to sharpen our sensitivity toward sin, let us confess our sins. I can say at the very least that confessing sin will help us to hate sin.

Is there any controversy between you and other people? In the diary of Pastor Cook, it was written: "There is nothing between me and men, I now have nothing to repent, nothing to recompense; I am prepared to die." Can we also say that we have confessed all our sins? Is there anyone who has yet to make confession? How often people dare not settle accounts. This by itself unveils the fact that there is something wrong. As we are about to eat a pear, and notice a small hole in the skin, we sense that something may be wrong inside that fruit. We may want to eat the pear but we are afraid to open it up.

The scope of confession is governed by the scope of sin. Do not confess more than the scope of sin, nor confess less than its scope. If the scope of my sin is that I have offended God, I must confess to God as my scope of confession. But if I sin against both God and a certain brother, then my scope of confession must include both God and that brother. It is therefore unwise to confess openly to the public what I have sinned against God or another person.

In many revival meetings, people are asked to confess their sins in public. This is a mistake, for it only defiles many minds. Confess to one person if the sin is against one person; confess to five persons if the sin is against five persons. On the other hand, the scope of confession should not be less than the scope of sin. If I sin against God and also against another brother, it is not acceptable just to confess to God and not to that brother. Confessions ought not be any wider or narrower than those who have been offended by the sin.

—*Grace for Grace*

QUESTIONS TO CONSIDER
1. When was the last time you confessed your sin to God?
2. How can you learn to more readily confess your sin?

A PRAYERFUL RESPONSE
Lord, today I will confess my sin to You. Amen.

DAY 8

Living by Faith

THOUGHT FOR TODAY

God teaches His children to live by faith.

WISDOM FROM SCRIPTURE

I am not ashamed of the gospel, because it is the power of God for the salvation of everyone who believes: first for the Jew, then for the Gentile.

For in the gospel a righteousness from God is revealed, a righteousness that is by faith from first to last, just as it is written: "The righteous will live by faith."

Therefore, since we have been justified through faith, we have peace with God through our Lord Jesus Christ, through whom we have gained access by faith into this grace in which we now stand. And we rejoice in the hope of the glory of God.

Not only so, but we also rejoice in our sufferings, because we know that suffering produces perseverance; perseverance, character; and character, hope.

And hope does not disappoint us, because God has poured out his love into our hearts by the Holy Spirit, whom he has given us.

ROMANS 1:16-17; 5:1-5, NIV

INSIGHTS FROM WATCHMAN NEE

Today God has this purpose that the just shall live by faith and not live by feeling. However we may feel, that does not give us anything. With some believers, God has to train them not to live by their emotional strength. He allows their dryness to grow longer and intensify deeper so as to lead them to the place where they can live by faith. If you have never been trained, you will soon discover how utterly powerless your emotional strength is. For the just shall live by faith alone.

If you do learn to live by faith, you may live the most joyous life in the midst of aridity—and the most tasteless life in the midst of felicity. This may sound paradoxical, yet this is a truth in spiritual life. God will lead us to live the life of faith.

What is meant by living by faith? It is represented to us very clearly by the words spoken to Nebuchadnezzar by the Hebrews Shadrach, Meshach and Abednego: "Our God whom we serve is able to deliver us from the burning fiery furnace: and he will deliver us out of thy hand, O king. But if not, be it known unto thee, O king, that we will not serve thy gods, nor worship the golden image which thou hast set up" (Dn 3:17-18). What they meant was that even if God should not save them, they would not be affected, they would not change. That is what is meant to live by faith!

Christians nowadays incline too strongly towards a life of feeling. If God should take away their joyous feeling, they would lose everything. Yet God does not say to live by feeling, but He says to live by faith. After years of experience you will come to realize that joy and dryness are really the same. No great outburst of joy will affect you, nor will any moment of dryness influence you. You live the same life through deep aridity as well as through great joy.

Oh that we may not act like those with a small capacity—in joy they dance in the house; in dryness they drench the wall with tears. If we live by faith we shall not be swayed by either of them. Even so, let it be plainly understood that we are not people without emotion. We do have feelings of joy as well as of dryness. But we ought not allow these external sensations to touch our inward man; for … the joy the outward man feels is not that which the inward man enjoys in the Lord, because this latter joy is most deep and unshakable. Yet this deep and unshakable joy is not experienced fully until we are able to control this outward joy. May the Lord be able to achieve His aims in us so that we may live by faith and not by feeling.

—*The Salvation of the Soul*

QUESTIONS TO CONSIDER
1. Do you live more by faith or by feeling? How do you know?
2. How can you focus more on faith responses?

A PRAYERFUL RESPONSE
Lord, I ask for Your faith to make decisions today. Amen.

The Light of God's Word

THOUGHT FOR TODAY

We can bask in the light of God's Word.

WISDOM FROM SCRIPTURE

Now the Lord is the Spirit, and where the Spirit of the Lord is, there is freedom.

And we, who with unveiled faces all reflect the Lord's glory, are being transformed into his likeness with ever-increasing glory, which comes from the Lord, who is the Spirit.

Therefore, since through God's mercy we have this ministry, we do not lose heart.

Rather, we have renounced secret and shameful ways; we do not use deception, nor do we distort the word of God. On the contrary, by setting forth the truth plainly we commend ourselves to every man's conscience in the sight of God.

And even if our gospel is veiled, it is veiled to those who are perishing.

The god of this age has blinded the minds of unbelievers, so that they cannot see the light of the gospel of the glory of Christ, who is the image of God.

For we do not preach ourselves, but Jesus Christ as Lord, and ourselves as your servants for Jesus' sake.

For God, who said, "Let light shine out of darkness," made his light shine in our hearts to give us the light of the knowledge of the glory of God in the face of Christ.

2 CORINTHIANS 3:17-18; 4:1-6, NIV

The Bible is the Word of God. It is full of God's light. This light is to enlighten all whose hearts are open to Him. "But we all, with unveiled face beholding as in a mirror the glory of the Lord" (2 Cor 3:18). Beholding the Lord with unveiled face is a basic condition to being enlightened by glory. If anyone approaches the Lord with veiled face, how can he expect the glory of the Lord to shine on him? God's light shines on only those who are open to Him. Unless one is open to God, he has no way of obtaining His light. The problem lies in his being closed to God. His spirit, his heart, his will, and his mind are all closed to Him, and hence he will not have the light of the Bible to shine on him.

It is just like the sun which, being so full of light, is meant to enlighten the inhabited world; but if we sit in the house with all doors and windows shut, its light is not able to enter and shine upon us. The difficulty is not with the light, but with the person. Light can only illumine those who are open to it. Now if this is true in the case of physical light it is equally true with spiritual light. Whenever we close ourselves up, light is prevented from lightening us.

Some believers are closed to God, and they will therefore never see His light. Instead of only spending time on reading, let us also examine ourselves as to whether we are open to God. If our face is veiled, the glory of the Lord is unable to illumine us. If our heart is not open to God, how can He give us light?

Light has its precise law. It enlightens all who are open to it. The measure of openness determines the amount of illumination. Even if we should shut all doors and windows of a room, the physical light will still in some measure penetrate should there be any fissures. Consequently, it is not difficult to receive light. Simply follow this law of openness, and you will have light. Whereas, if this law of light is violated, then there can be no light whatsoever.

The one who is closed to God cannot be a person who knows the Bible, regardless how much research he engages in or how long he prays. It is extremely hard for anyone to expect enlightenment with a closed heart. God's light is not given unconditionally to man. For man to obtain God's light, he must fulfill its condition.

Although all the children of God have the same Bible, the enlightenment they receive from it varies greatly. Some seem to have no understanding of the Book at all, some receive a little light, while still others find it full of light. The reason for such variation lies in the readers. The light of God remains the same, but people themselves are not the same. Some are open to God, so they are able to understand the Bible; but others are closed to God, hence they are not able to understand. Some people's closure is complete, therefore their darkness is likewise total; while the closure of others is partial and consequently the light they receive is partial.

Whatever may be the degree of incapability to see—whether large or small, whole or partial—it all proves the darkness within us. Never think for a moment that to study the Bible well or not is an insignificant matter. If a person does not study the Bible well, it indicates one fact—this man lives in darkness! How very serious it is for a person not to be able to understand God's Word and see the light therein.

The question may be asked, What exactly is meant by being open to God? This openness must come from a consecration which is unconditional and without reservation. To be open to God is not a temporary attitude; it is a permanent characteristic before Him. It is not occasional, it is continuous. If one's consecration to God is perfect and absolute, his attitude towards God will naturally be unreserved, and nowhere in him is he closed to God. Any indication of closure only points to the imperfection of one's consecration. All darkness comes from closure, and all closure comes from lack of consecration.

Wherever consecration is lacking there is a place of reservation. Where one is unable to yield to God, there he must defend himself; and in that area he has no way to the truth of the Bible. For when he comes to that area, he will only circle around and around it. Simply stated, then, darkness arises out of closure, and closure stems from lack of consecration.

—*Ye Search the Scriptures*

QUESTIONS TO CONSIDER
1. In what areas of your life are you open to God's light?
2. How can you be more open to God through His Word?

A PRAYERFUL RESPONSE
Lord, help me to be more open to Your light and truth. Amen.

Treasure in a Vessel

THOUGHT FOR TODAY

Though we are weak vessels, God fills us with His strength.

WISDOM FROM SCRIPTURE

But we have this treasure in jars of clay to show that this all-surpassing power is from God and not from us.

We are hard pressed on every side, but not crushed; perplexed, but not in despair; persecuted, but not abandoned; struck down, but not destroyed.

We always carry around in our body the death of Jesus, so that the life of Jesus may also be revealed in our body.

For we who are alive are always being given over to death for Jesus' sake, so that his life may be revealed in our mortal body.

So then, death is at work in us, but life is at work in you.

Therefore we do not lose heart. Though outwardly we are wasting away, yet inwardly we are being renewed day by day.

For our light and momentary troubles are achieving for us an eternal glory that far outweighs them all.

So we fix our eyes not on what is seen, but on what is unseen. For what is seen is temporary, but what is unseen is eternal.

2 CORINTHIANS 4:7-12, 16-18, NIV

"We also have this treasure in earthen vessels." This is possibly the clearest statement there is of the nature of practical Christianity. Christianity is not the earthen vessel, nor is it the treasure, but it is the treasure in the earthen vessel.

All people, whether Christians or not, have their ideal man. All have their own particular conceptions of what constitutes a good man. They think that if a man does such-and-such things, or behaves in some particular way, or if he is a certain kind of person, that man is good. We have each a set standard in our minds, and if a man measures up to that we call him a "good" man. Before we were saved we had a certain standard, but of course after our salvation we came to see that many whom we admired before were not really to be admired. We judge them now by our newfound light, and we see that they come short. Our scale of measurement has altered.

To be a Christian is to be a person in whom seeming incompatibles exist together, but in whom it is the power of God that repeatedly triumphs. A Christian is one in whose life there is inherent a mysterious paradox, and this paradox is of God. Some people conceive of Christianity as being all treasure and no vessel. If sometimes the earthen vessel is evident in a servant of God, they feel he is a hopeless case, whereas God's conception is that in that very vessel His treasure should be found.

How can the Lord's power be manifested to perfection in a weak man? By Christianity; for Christianity is that very thing. Christianity is not the removal of weakness, nor is it merely the manifestation of divine power. It is the manifestation of divine power in the presence of human weakness.

Let us be clear on this point. What the Lord is doing is no merely negative thing—that is to say, the elimination of our infirmity. Nor, for that matter, is it merely positive—the bestowal of strength at random. No, He leaves us with the infirmity, and He bestows the strength there. He is bestowing His strength upon men, but that strength is manifested in their weakness. All the treasure He gives is placed in earthen vessels.

—*What Shall This Man Do?*

QUESTIONS TO CONSIDER

1. When have you been weak, and God was strong?
2. How do you need God's strength today?

A PRAYERFUL RESPONSE

Lord, thank You that when I am weak, then You are strong. Amen.

PART TWO

Conformed to His Image

O to be like Thee! blessed Redeemer,
This is my constant longing and prayer.
Gladly I'll forfeit all of earth's treasures,
Jesus, Thy perfect likeness to wear.

O to be like Thee! O to be like Thee,
Blessed Redeemer, pure as Thou art!
Come in Thy sweetness, come in Thy fullness;
Stamp Thine own image deep on my heart.

"O TO BE LIKE THEE!"
BY THOMAS O. CHISHOLM

WATCHMAN NEE'S INSIGHT
Becoming like Christ begins with transforming the heart.

How Is Your Heart?

THOUGHT FOR TODAY

God is looking for people after His own heart.

WISDOM FROM SCRIPTURE

The law of the LORD is perfect, reviving the soul;

the decrees of the LORD are sure, making wise the simple;

the precepts of the LORD are right, rejoicing the heart;

the commandment of the LORD is clear, enlightening the eyes;

the fear of the LORD is pure, enduring forever;

the ordinances of the LORD are true and righteous altogether.

More to be desired are they than gold, even much fine gold;

sweeter also than honey, and drippings of the honeycomb.

Moreover by them is your servant warned; in keeping them there is great reward.

But who can detect their errors? Clear me from hidden faults.

Keep back your servant also from the insolent; do not let them have dominion over me.

Then I shall be blameless, and innocent of great transgression.

PSALM 19:7-13, NRSV

What kind of man is a man after God's own heart? It is the one who allows God to touch his heart. If a person will not allow Him to touch his heart, he can hardly be a man after God's own heart.

Many Christians tend to ask: Am I not right in doing so and so? Am I not right in speaking thus? Am I not correct in such expression? Yet the essential question does not lie in whether their doing or speaking or expressing is right or not; it rests instead upon what is the root of their doing, speaking or expressing. Even though a person is all right outwardly, he may still have a problem with his heart. What God will ask about, and touch, will concern itself with that one's heart. It is for this reason that He permits many things to happen—wave upon wave—in the lives of His children. He uses these things to touch their hearts by exposing what is there.

God's children must not only be careful about their speech and attitude; even more so, they should be careful of the thought and intent of their hearts. Frequently our outward expression does not necessarily reveal the inward condition. More often than not it is our inner feeling which betrays the real condition of our heart. How futile it is merely to keep a guard over our lips. If our heart is not right, sooner or later, it will be openly expressed—and often when we least expect it.

An example of this would be our idle words spoken about other people. The more our heart is toward God, and the purer it is to Him, the fewer will be the idle words we shall utter. Every time we gossip and murmur against people we betray some irregularity in our heart. For if a person's heart were wholly towards God, he would not say such idle words against other people.

A brother once said, "If a little brother sins against me, I can forgive him, but if a big brother sins against me, I cannot forgive him." Another brother who heard him say this looked at the chest of this brother and nodded his head continuously. What he meant by this gesture was: "Your heart! Your heart! In forgiving a little brother but in not forgiving a big brother, you expose what your heart is like. The fact that a little brother sins against you and is forgiven by you cannot at all expose your true heart condition; but when you refuse to forgive a big brother who sins against you, that really reveals what is in your heart." Through this incident, that brother's unforgiving heart was unveiled. Let us see that something small may not be burned by a single match, but it will be completely consumed in a fiery furnace. This shows that this thing can be burned. Similarly speaking, a little brother was not able to test out this brother's heart, but a big brother was instrumental in bringing out what was truly his inward state.

If our heart is right, we will not be shaken by anybody, for we look only to God. David proved to be a man after God's own heart because in whatever environment God placed him, his heart was kept in direct relationship with the Lord and not with men. David accepted everything from God's hand and tried to see things from His viewpoint.

Let me repeat that God uses circumstances to reveal our heart. May we therefore pray: "O Lord, let the words of my mouth and the meditations of my heart be acceptable in Your sight."

—*The Messenger of the Cross*

QUESTIONS TO CONSIDER

1. Based on your recent actions, what is the condition of your heart?

2. How might you allow God to more deeply touch your heart?

A PRAYERFUL RESPONSE

Lord, I want my heart to reflect Your heart. Amen.

The Purpose of Brokenness

THOUGHT FOR TODAY

God uses pain to make us more like Him.

WISDOM FROM SCRIPTURE

Create in me a clean heart, O God,
    and put a new and right spirit within me.
    Do not cast me away from your presence,
    and do not take your holy spirit from me.
    Restore to me the joy of your salvation,
    and sustain in me a willing spirit.
    Then I will teach transgressors your ways,
    and sinners will return to you.
    Deliver me from bloodshed, O God,
    O God of my salvation,
    and my tongue will sing aloud of your deliverance.

O LORD, open my lips,
    and my mouth will declare your praise,
    For you have no delight in sacrifice;
    if I were to give a burnt offering,
    you would not be pleased.
    The sacrifice acceptable to God is a broken spirit;
    a broken and contrite heart, O God, you will not despise.

PSALM 51:10-17, NRSV

Since the Holy Spirit works according to the light of God, His discipline is thorough and complete. We often wonder at the things that befall us, yet if left to ourselves we may be mistaken in our very best choice. The discipline He orders transcends our understanding. How often we are caught unprepared and conclude that surely such a drastic thing is not our need. Many times His discipline descends upon us suddenly without our having prior notice! We may insist we are living in "the light," but the Holy Spirit is dealing with us according to God's light. From the time we received Him, He has been ordering our circumstances for our profit, according to His knowledge of us.

The working of the Holy Spirit in our lives has its positive as well as its negative side—that is to say, there is both a constructive and a destructive phase. After we are born again the Holy Spirit dwells in us, but our outward man so often deprives Him of His freedom. It is like trying to walk in a pair of ill-fitting shoes. Because our outward and inward man are at variance with each other, God must employ whatever means He thinks effective in breaking down any stronghold over which our inward man has no control.

It is not by the supply of grace to this inward man that the Holy Spirit breaks the outward. Of course, God wants the inward man to be strong, but His method is to utilize external means to decrease our outward man. It would be well nigh impossible for the inward man to accomplish this, since these two are so different in nature that they can scarcely inflict any wound on each other. The nature of the outward man and that of external things are similar, and thus the former can be easily affected by the latter. External things can strike the outward man most painfully. So it is that God uses external things in dealing with our outward man.

You remember the Bible says that two sparrows are sold for a farthing (see Mt 10:29) and that five sparrows are sold for two farthings (see Lk 12:6). This is certainly cheap, and the fifth sparrow is included free. However, "One of them shall not fall on the ground without your Father; but the very hairs of your head are all numbered" (see Mt 10:29, 30). Not only is every hair counted, but every single one is also numbered. Hence we may be sure that all our circumstances are ordered by God. Nothing is accidental.

God's ordering is according to His knowledge of our needs, and with a view to the shattering of our outward man. Knowing that a certain external thing will thus affect us, He arranges for us to encounter it once, twice, and perhaps even more. Do you not realize that all the events of your life for the past five or ten years were ordered by God for your education? If you murmured and complained, you grievously failed to recognize His hand. If you thought you were just unfortunate, you were in ignorance of the discipline of the Holy Spirit.

Remember that whatever happens to us is measured by the hand of God for our supreme good. Though probably it is not what we would choose, God knows what is best for us. Where would we be today had God not so disciplined us through ordering our circumstances? It is this which keeps us pure and walking in His pathway. How foolish are those who have murmuring in their mouths and rebellion in their hearts at the things the Holy Spirit has measured to them for their good.

—*The Release of the Spirit*

QUESTIONS TO CONSIDER

1. In what ways has your "outer self" been broken?
2. How has this changed your relationship with God?

A PRAYERFUL RESPONSE

Lord, I offer the pain and brokenness of my life to You. Amen.

Flesh or Spirit?

THOUGHT FOR TODAY

The Spirit can win the battle over the flesh.

WISDOM FROM SCRIPTURE

I do not understand my own actions. For I do not do what I want, but I do the very thing I hate.

Now if I do what I do not want, I agree that the law is good.

But in fact it is no longer I that do it, but sin that dwells within me.

For I know that nothing good dwells within me, that is, in my flesh. I can will what is right, but I cannot do it.

For I do not do the good I want, but the evil I do not want is what I do.

Now if I do what I do not want, it is no longer I that do it, but sin that dwells within me.

So I find it to be a law that when I want to do what is good, evil lies close at hand.

For I delight in the law of God in my inmost self, but I see in my members another law at war with the law of my mind, making me captive to the law of sin that dwells in my members.

ROMANS 7:15-23, NRSV

INSIGHTS FROM WATCHMAN NEE

God's purpose is not in reforming the flesh, but in destroying its vital center. In giving His life to man at the time of regeneration, God intends to use this life to destroy the self of the flesh. Although this life given by God to man is most powerful, in a newborn babe in Christ it is at first rather feeble. For the flesh has long held sway, and the newly born has not exercised faith to lay hold of God's perfect salvation. So that during this initial period, though he is born again, he is yet carnal.

By carnality is meant that he is yet under the control of the flesh. What is most to be pitied is the fact that being born again, he already has the heavenly light shining in him. So he knows how wicked is the flesh and he desires with all his heart to overcome the flesh. But due to the feebleness of his inner strength, he cannot do what he wants to do.

During this period he sheds many tears. In fact, every born-again child of God possesses this new desire of destroying sin in order to please God. Yet the will is not strong enough to overcome the flesh. Consequently, he experiences more defeats than he does victories. How deplorable is such a time!

The experience Paul describes in Romans 7 is the history of such a battle. His final sigh is this: "Wretched man that I am! Who shall deliver me out of the body of this death?" How this sigh finds response in many hearts!

What does such battling really mean? Such battling is also a kind of discipline of the Holy Spirit. For God has already provided for man's perfect redemption. Man fails to obtain this so great salvation not because he does not know it but because he wills not to have it. For this reason, when a person asks for forgiveness at the time of regeneration, he is given by God both forgiveness and regeneration. Then subsequently, through such battling as we have already described, God induces a believer to seek and to lay hold of the complete victory.

In case a believer fails to have victory due to the lack of knowledge, such struggling he experiences will urge him onward to seek to know, and the Holy Spirit will have the opportunity to reveal to him how Christ has already on the cross dealt with his old man, so that he will be led to believe and to possess. But if he wills not for such possession, the truth will remain in his mind until he discovers that knowledge alone will not help him in the battle. Many defeats may then eventually cause him to long to experience the truth he already knows.

Such battling will increase as the days go on. If a believer does not fall into despair, but advances forward faithfully, he will experience even more severe fightings. For such severe struggle will not cease until he finds deliverance. But deliverance will indeed come at last.

—*The Spirit of Judgment*

QUESTIONS TO CONSIDER
1. Do you identify with Paul's struggle against the flesh?
2. What steps can you take to be more controlled by the Spirit?

A PRAYERFUL RESPONSE
Lord, help me to be Spirit-controlled today. Amen.

Chosen by God

THOUGHT FOR TODAY

God chooses us to do His work in the world.

WISDOM FROM SCRIPTURE

"So come, I will send you to Pharaoh to bring my people, the Israelites, out of Egypt."

But Moses said to God, "Who am I that I should go to Pharaoh, and bring the Israelites out of Egypt?"

He said, "I will be with you; and this shall be the sign for you that it is I who sent you: when you have brought the people out of Egypt, you shall worship God on this mountain."

But Moses said to God, "If I come to the Israelites and say to them, 'The God of your ancestors has sent me to you' and they ask me, 'What is his name?' what shall I say to them?"

God said to Moses, "I AM WHO I AM." He said further, "Thus you shall say to the Israelites, 'I AM has sent me to you.'"

God also said to Moses, "Thus you shall say to the Israelites, 'The LORD, the God of your ancestors, the God of Abraham, the God of Isaac, and the God of Jacob, has sent me to you.

"'This is my name forever,

'and this is my title for all generations.'"

But Moses said to the LORD, "O my Lord, I have never been eloquent, neither in the past nor even now that you have spoken to your servant; but I am slow of speech and slow of tongue."

Then the LORD said to him, "Who gives speech to mortals?

Who makes them mute or deaf, seeing or blind? Is it not I, the LORD?

"Now go, and I will be with your mouth and teach you what you are to speak."

EXODUS 3:10-15; 4:10-12, NRSV

INSIGHTS FROM WATCHMAN NEE

Moses was the first servant chosen by God. He was the first person called by God to service. Though Abraham, Isaac and Jacob lived before the time of Moses, they were not, strictly speaking, God's servants. They were not covenanted with God as such. Just as Paul may be considered the first servant chosen by God in New Testament times, so Moses may be reckoned as His first chosen servant in the Old Testament period.

How did God deal with Moses? In what way did Moses please Him? Before He could deal with the children of Israel, God had first to deal with Moses. Before He could deal with the pharaoh and the Egyptians, He had to deal with Moses.

A servant of the Lord once wrote: "When man thinks of doing something, he always thinks of the way of doing it; but when God intends to do a thing, He usually tries first of all to find the man." Except He finds the right person, God has no way. Today in the church we have all kinds of ways, places and organizations available, but do we have men? For God does not lay stress on the way, but the man. How very different is man's idea from God's. People assume that a good method will lead to a satisfactory result. Yet they fail to consider the person who executes the method; consequently, they are not able to obtain the good fruit they expect.

The issue, of course, is not that God cannot find people with great talents today; what He cannot find are people who are usable. Three months after he was born, Moses was placed in the water. He was later pulled out of the water by the daughter of Pharaoh, who adopted him as her son. Hence the name was given to him of "Moses," which means "the drawing out of water." He was the first one drawn out. Later on, the multitudes of the children of Israel would follow his train by being drawn out themselves (the Red Sea experience).

In the wilderness, God dealt with Moses first, and then in the same wilderness He dealt with the children of Israel after they had been led out of Egypt by Moses. Unless we are delivered, we cannot expect other people to be delivered. If we do not have a vision, how can we expect others to see God's way? Except we walk in it, no one else will be able to follow. Today God wishes to deal with us first. And after He has gotten some of us, we can then expect to gain other people.

Unless God is able to use you, He has no way. If the Holy Spirit has no opportunity to fill you, He cannot work through you to bring salvation to others. You will simply have no power to work, because His power and life have no way to flow out. Only through you can His riches be manifested. In order to be a person whom God can use, you must do two things: trust and obey.

God had made a covenant with Abraham, Isaac and Jacob to deliver their descendants. He saw how the children of Israel were ill-treated by the Egyptians, and He heard their cry. So He intended to save them according to the covenant He had made with them. But please realize that in order for God to save the people, He must first find a channel that could act as a liaison between Him and the people He would save. He must first obtain His channel, and then He can work.

Moses was the channel God used, and he did not fail Him. God was able to use him mightily. Today, how many believers have disappointed the Lord because He cannot use them? God is currently looking everywhere to find the man whom He needs and whom He can use.

—A Balanced Christian Life

QUESTIONS TO CONSIDER

1. Are you willing to be chosen by God for His purposes?
2. How can you be a more willing vessel for God?

A PRAYERFUL RESPONSE

Lord, I offer myself as Your chosen servant to carry out Your purpose and will. Amen.

DAY 15

Death to Self

THOUGHT FOR TODAY
Through death to self we find true life in Christ.

WISDOM FROM SCRIPTURE
And he told them many things in parables, saying: "Listen! A sower went out to sow.

"And as he sowed, some seeds fell on the path, and the birds came and ate them up.

"Other seeds fell on rocky ground, where they did not have much soil, and they sprang up quickly, since they had no depth of soil.

"But when the sun rose, they were scorched; and since they had no root, they withered away.

"Other seeds fell among thorns, and the thorns grew up and choked them.

"Other seeds fell on good soil and brought forth grain, some a hundredfold, some sixty, some thirty.

"Let anyone with ears listen!"

He answered, "The one who sows the good seed is the Son of Man; the field is the world, and the good seed are the children of the kingdom; the weeds are the children of the evil one, and the enemy who sowed them is the devil; the harvest is the end of the age, and the reapers are angels.

"Just as the weeds are collected and burned up with fire, so will it be at the end of the age.

"The Son of Man will send his angels, and they will collect

out of his kingdom all causes of sin and all evil-doers, and they will throw them into the furnace of fire, where there will be weeping and gnashing of teeth.

"Then the righteous will shine like the sun in the kingdom of their Father. Let anyone with ears listen!"

MATTHEW 13:3-9, 37-43, NRSV

INSIGHTS FROM WATCHMAN NEE

Let us not despise the word "die." It is not enough simply to be a grain of wheat. To be a regenerated child (see Mt 13:8, 38) is merely to be a newborn baby who can at first do little, if anything, for God. Neither is it enough only to fall into the ground, for though we may be willing to suffer and to be hidden, we remain as one grain without any increase if we do not die. Death is the final, decisive step. Death is the door to life. Death is the only way to fruitfulness. Death is absolutely necessary.

But how many of us are really dead? Death is the cessation of all movement. Once having died, the self can no longer be active. It is the end of man's day. Nonetheless, this death is not something forced, because the Lord declares that this life must be hated. Hate is an attitude, a sustained attitude. For this reason, we must willingly deliver this life to death, fully recognizing its deficiency and hating it with all our heart.

What, though, is the result of the dying of this life? "Much fruit." The reason—the only reason—why our Lord cannot use us is because our soul life with its intellect, affection, and so forth is of an inferior order which cannot bear any spiritual fruit if we depend on it. Although there are many of what we would consider to be good points surrounding the self life, nevertheless, our Lord Jesus makes clear that only "that which is born of the Spirit is spirit" (Jn 3:6). The self life, with all that it includes, can be of no help there. But in the event of our truly delivering ourselves—delivering our life, and all that we are capable of and all that we are—to the cross of Christ, we shall then see how God can use us. If we truly empty of ourselves, the living water of God can and will flow from us without any blockage. And such fruit bearing as this is out of the ordinary.

Therefore, even as our self filled us in the past, let us now let Christ fill us; otherwise, we will not have obtained full salvation. The turning point in anyone's full salvation is in that one being delivered from self. A self-centered believer is prone to fall into sin. To be wholly dead to sin demands of us that we also die to self. Christ is not only the Savior from our sins, He is also the Savior from ourselves. To die to the self life is the only pathway to spiritual life.

Only God can cause us to die to self; nobody else is able to. But if we are not willing, then this cannot be done even by God Himself. The words of the self life are sometimes very subtle, they being covered over or hidden by a spiritual veil. It is beyond the discernment of the believer. So much so that God will have to use outside circumstances to break through such a heavy veil and cause the believer to know his own self.

Self-knowledge is extremely rare. We do not know ourselves, at least not until we have been tried by God's hand and been shown the wickedness of our self life. If we have no experience of the death of self, our spiritual life will have little real progress. However, if we are willing from now on to let the Spirit of the Lord work the dying of self in us, then we will be able to live out a life in the Spirit.

Let us all say with one accord what our Lord Jesus prayed to His heavenly Father: "Not my will, but thine be done" (Lk 22:42).

—*Back to the Cross*

QUESTIONS TO CONSIDER

1. For you, what would it mean to die to self?
2. In what ways would you like to bear fruit for God?

A PRAYERFUL RESPONSE

Lord, I release my self-will in exchange for Your life-giving will. Amen.

DAY 16

A New Reaction

We can love those who hate us and bless those who curse us.

WISDOM FROM SCRIPTURE

"You have heard that it was said, 'Eye for eye, and tooth for tooth.'

"But I tell you, Do not resist an evil person. If someone strikes you on the right cheek, turn to him the other also.

"And if someone wants to sue you and take your tunic, let him have your cloak as well.

"If someone forces you to go one mile, go with him two miles.

"Give to the one who asks you, and do not turn away from the one who wants to borrow from you.

"You have heard that it was said, 'Love your neighbor and hate your enemy.'

"But I tell you: Love your enemies and pray for those who persecute you, that you may be sons of your Father in heaven. He causes his sun to rise on the evil and the good, and sends rain on the righteous and the unrighteous.

"If you love those who love you, what reward will you get? Are not even the tax collectors doing that?

"And if you greet only your brothers, what are you doing more than others? Do not even pagans do that?

"Be perfect, therefore, as your heavenly Father is perfect."

MATTHEW 5:38-48, NIV

Which is better—to smite or be smitten? Do you admire the way of most people? Because they smite others, would you do the same? Let me tell you, he who smites others is not acting as a Christian.

If you are struck by a brother today, do you know what he is giving you? He is giving you a great opportunity—one which cannot be better—to be enlarged as a Christian. Suppose your reaction is: How dare that brother hit me? How unreasonable he is! If your reaction is that, will you not then be tempted to strike back? Such a reaction is unchristian. When that brother smites you, you know immediately that he is not acting as a Christian, but at the same time you also realize that he has given you a fine opportunity to react like one.

All who smite others have lost their Christian dignity. Let us not admire them. But let us also remember that each time people ill-treat us, speak evil of us, or make unreasonable demands of us, they are giving us an opportunity to react as Christians. It is as if they are saying: "I am not going to be Christian in action, but I will let you!"

If a brother should sue you in court and try to take any money or clothing from you, he is telling you that he is no longer acting as a Christian but that he will let you do so. He forfeits his Christian ground but puts you on that ground. Should you not, then, thank God for the opportunity? You should say, "O God, I thank You and I praise You, because You put me on Christian ground. This, indeed, is Your grace." If you fall to the level of hitting back, you are finished. You lose your Christian ground and give others that opportunity. Therefore, brothers and sisters should strive to stand on Christian ground.

Once I had a certain transaction with a brother. I owed him nothing but he asked me for a large sum of money. My first reaction was that of irritation. How could he be a Christian and be so unreasonable? This was really too low. Could a righteous person make such a demand? But a second reaction came to me. I was happy; I was happy to give to him even though he was wrong. So I answered him, "Brother, do you really want the money?" He answered, "I do." It was at that time that the Lord gave me the word, "He is giving you an opportunity to be an enlarged Christian." This was the first time the Lord spoke this to me. Consequently, I prepared the money and gave it to him.

Since that day I have learned a lesson. When people act like that brother, they withdraw themselves from Christian ground, yet they give us an opportunity to be on that ground. If, under such circumstances, we too withdraw from Christian ground, it is most shameful and pitiable. We need to learn to say, "The Lord has put us on this ground that we may have the opportunity to be Christian in action." We will tell the Lord, "Lord, I want to act like a Christian." No loss can be greater than not being Christian in action.

To be smitten is a great loss; to be deprived of things is a great loss; to suffer disgrace is a great loss; to lose freedom is a great loss. But may I tell you, in allowing these things the Lord shows His confidence in you, wanting you to manifest His grace. You are to manifest not merely His power but also His grace and His generosity toward people. If we fail in this, how very great is the loss.

People may think it is the strong who smite others; but I say the strong is able to be smitten and not strike back. He who is unable to control his temper is weak; but he who can restrain himself is strong. The smitten one is the strong one; the one who turns his left cheek is really strong. He is strong because he can turn his left cheek and smite himself. Let us learn to know what is of spiritual value before God, not just of worldly value. Do not live by worldly standards, but live by spiritual standards.

I, therefore, desire all new believers to know what the Christian reaction is. Do not wait for three, five, eight, or ten years before you get on the road. Do not take the Teaching on the Mount as something too difficult. No Christian ought to delay learning the Teaching on the Mount. He should learn it as soon as he believes in the Lord, for the Teaching on the Mount is the first teaching. It stands right at the front door; it is not something that you see after having gone on with the Lord for some years. The Teaching on the Mount is the Christian's basic reaction; it is a reaction according to Christian nature. No spiritual progress is required to have this reaction. As soon as you believe in the Lord Jesus, you have such reactions. You will naturally have this experience. When you walk the second mile, your heart is joyful. Only by so doing are you comfortable and happy within.

—Not I But Christ

QUESTIONS TO CONSIDER
1. What situations provoke you to "fight back"?
2. Specifically and practically, how can you love and bless those who attack you?

A PRAYERFUL RESPONSE
Lord, help me to offer Your response when I feel attacked. Amen.

Bearing the Cross

THOUGHT FOR TODAY

Through God's loving discipline we learn to respond to Him.

WISDOM FROM SCRIPTURE

Happy are those who make the Lord their trust,
who do not turn to the proud,
to those who go astray after false gods.
You have multiplied, O Lord my God,
your wondrous deeds and your thoughts toward us;
none can compare with you.
Were I to proclaim and tell of them,
they would be more than can be counted.
Sacrifice and offering you do not desire,
but you have given me an open ear.
Burnt offering and sin offering you have not required.
Then I said, "Here I am;
in the scroll of the book it is written of me;
I delight to do your will, O my God;
your law is within my heart."
I have told the glad news of deliverance
in the great congregation;
see, I have not restrained my lips,
as you know, O Lord.
I have not hidden your saving help within my heart,
I have spoken of your faithfulness and your salvation;
I have not concealed your steadfast love and your
   faithfulness from the great congregation.

PSALM 40:4-10, NRSV

God is bringing you to the place where He has but to express a wish and you respond instantly. That is the spirit of the servant (see Ps 40:7-8), but such a spirit does not come naturally to any of us. It comes only when our soul, the seat of our natural energy and will and affections, has been brought, by the touch of the Cross, under His sway. Yet such a servant spirit is what He seeks, and will have in us all. The way to it may be long-drawn, or it may be just one stroke; but God has His ways and we must have regard for them.

Every true servant of God must know at some time that disabling from which he can never recover; he can never be quite the same again. There must be that established in you which means that from henceforth you will really fear yourself. You will fear to move out on the impulse of your soul, for you know what a bad time you will have in your heart before the Lord if you do. You have known something of the chastening hand of a loving God upon you, a God who "dealeth with us as with sons" (Heb 12:7). The Spirit Himself bears witness in our spirits to that relationship, and to the inheritance and glory that are ours "if so be that we suffer with him" (Rom 8:17) and your response to the Father of our spirits is, "Abba, Father" (Rom 8:15).

But when this is really established in you, you have come to a new place which we speak of as "resurrection ground." Death, in principle, may have had to be wrought out to a crisis in your natural life, but when it has, then you find God releases you into resurrection. You discover that what you have lost is being given back, though not quite as before. The principle of life is at work in you now: something that directs and empowers you, animating you with fresh divine life. From henceforth what you have lost will be brought back, but touched now with new values under heaven's control.

Let me make this clear. If we want to be spiritual people, there is no need for us to amputate our hands or feet: we can still have our body. In the same way we can have our soul, with the full use of its faculties, and yet the soul is not now our life-spring. We are no longer living in it, we are no longer drawing from it and living by it; we use it. When the body becomes our life, we live like beasts. When the soul becomes our life, we live as rebels and fugitives from God—gifted, cultured, educated, no doubt, but alienated from the life of God. But when we come to live our life in the Spirit and by the Spirit, though we still use our soul faculties just as we do our physical faculties, they are now the servants of the Spirit; and when we have reached that point, God can really use us.

We would like to have death and resurrection put together within one hour of each other. We cannot face the thought that God will keep us aside for so long a time; we cannot bear to wait. And of course I cannot tell you how long He will take, but in principle I think it is quite safe to say this, that there will be a definite period when He will keep you there. It will seem as though nothing is happening; as though everything you valued is slipping from your grip. There confronts you a blank wall with no door in it. Seemingly, everyone else is being blessed and used, while you yourself have been passed by and are losing out.

Lie quiet. All is in darkness, but it is only for a night. It must indeed be a full night, but that is all. Afterwards you will find that everything is given back to you in glorious resurrection; and nothing can measure the difference between what was before and what now is!

—*The Normal Christian Life*

QUESTIONS TO CONSIDER

1. What could help you develop a servant spirit?
2. At what stage are you, in the death and resurrection process?

A PRAYERFUL RESPONSE

Lord, I exchange my desires for Your cross of service. Amen.

The Mind of Christ

THOUGHT FOR TODAY

As the body of Christ, we are to be of one mind—the mind of Christ.

WISDOM FROM SCRIPTURE

If then there is any encouragement from love, any sharing in the Spirit, any compassion and sympathy, make my joy complete: be of the same mind, having the same love, being in full accord and of one mind.

Do nothing from selfish ambition or conceit, but in humility regard others as better than yourselves.

Let each of you look not to your own interests, but to the interests of others.

Let the same mind be in you that was in Christ Jesus, who, though he was in the form of God, did not regard equality with God as something to be exploited, but emptied himself, taking the form of a slave, being born in human likeness.

And being found in human form, he humbled himself and became obedient to the point of death—even death on a cross.

Therefore God also highly exalted him and gave him the name that is above every name, so that at the name of Jesus every knee should bend, in heaven and on earth and under the earth, and every tongue should confess that Jesus Christ is Lord, to the glory of God the Father.

PHILIPPIANS 2:1-11, NRSV

Can there be the same mind? The same love? Once I asked a brother in Foochow the process whereby we two would be of the same mind. Would it be necessary for me to change my mind to his or for him to change his mind to mine? Now it might be possible with two persons, but what if there were three people involved? How could two people's minds be changed to the mind of the third person? And supposing there were five, or five hundred, or a thousand people involved, how could so many minds become the same?

Yet according to Paul, it would appear to be very easy for all to arrive at the same mind. For the apostle, it is simply as verse 5 suggests: "Have this mind in you, which was also in Christ Jesus." The solution to the problem is not to be found in the formula whereby I am to lay aside my mind in deference to yours, nor by you laying aside your mind in deference to my mind. It is instead achieved by our placing the mind of Christ in the midst of us, allowing both of us to be of the same mind with Him. If every mind is to be of the same mind as Christ's, then it is a matter of all of us simply having the same mind, in spite of the great number of people involved.

When we are attempting to undertake something, it is quite likely that you will have your thought and I will have mine. Should you, then, submit to me, or should I submit to you? Some people may think that perhaps the other person should submit. But this is not God's way. His way is to "have this mind in you which was also in Christ Jesus."

What loss it will be to God if any brother or sister should go astray and refuse to obey the Lord! Were we of the same mind, it would give God joy—yea, much joy; for here Paul is representing the Lord's heart. The heart of the Lord will be full of joy if believers are of one mind. A number of things can indeed gladden the Lord's heart, but the one accord of Christians will make Him full of joy. Winning souls will give the Lord joy; victorious living will also give Him joy; but having one mind will give Him great joy.

Such oneness is internal as well as external. God can so work in us that we are not only one in speech but also one in heart.

Some people's oneness is merely in their mouths, because their hearts are not really one. Even though their hearts are so far apart, and their attitudes betray the fact that they are not of one accord with other people, they can still declare they are one. Such oneness is not that which is spoken of here. Only on the basis of "If there is … in Christ" can there be any one-mindedness.

"Do nothing through faction or through vainglory, but in lowliness of mind each counting the other better than himself" (verse 3). This is still based on Paul's understanding of the phrase "in Christ." What is faction? Factionalism denotes the taking of sides. Instead of the Lord, someone else becomes your goal. When two persons are at odds, for example, you declare that you are for one of them. But this is wrong. You can only stand on the Lord's side, or else you will fall into factionalism.

What kind of glory is vainglory? The Scriptures at one point speak of an "eternal weight of glory" (2 Cor 4:17). Glory is weighty and substantial, therefore it sinks to the bottom; it doesn't float on the top. Such weight of glory can only be seen by God. What is apparent and seen by many people is something vainglorious. What does a person obtain from such vainglory? Nothing but a lusting, for who can ever obtain that which is vain and empty? All he can do is to lust continually after it.

Sometimes, unfortunate strife occurs among brothers and sisters. If this is not due to faction, then it usually is because of seeking after vainglory. Each desires to be great; none is willing to give in. Actually, desiring greatness will not make one great; there will always be someone greater.

When one is being praised and honored, he seems to be glorified, whereas in fact his feet tread on floating clouds. We need to remember that all glories that come from men are but vainglories. Who, then, is worthy to praise us? Apart from our Lord, no one is worthy. When we are praised by men, we have already been downgraded, so why should we lust after it? We will not accept men's praise nor seek for such praise if our mind is set on the future and our heart seeks to hear the Lord say, "Well done, good and faithful servant" (Mt 25:21).

—*From Glory to Glory*

QUESTIONS TO CONSIDER

1. How can you tell if you have the mind of Christ?
2. Do you need restoration with another believer? How can you express the mind of Christ to each other?

A PRAYERFUL RESPONSE

Lord, let me be of one mind with You today. Amen.

Matters of Authority

THOUGHT FOR TODAY

God calls us to submit to the authority He has placed over us.

WISDOM FROM SCRIPTURE

He began to tell the people this parable: "A man planted a vineyard, and leased it to tenants, and went to another country for a long time.

"When the season came, he sent a slave to the tenants in order that they might give him his share of the produce of the vineyard; but the tenants beat him and sent him away empty-handed.

"Next he sent another slave; that one also they beat and insulted and sent away empty-handed.

"And he sent still a third; this one also they wounded and threw out.

"Then the owner of the vineyard said, 'What shall I do? I will send my beloved son; perhaps they will respect him.'

"But when the tenants saw him, they discussed it among themselves and said, 'This is the heir; let us kill him so that the inheritance may be ours.'

"So they threw him out of the vineyard and killed him. What then will the owner of the vineyard do to them?

"He will come and destroy those tenants and give the vineyard to others." When they heard this, they said, "Heaven forbid!"

LUKE 20:9-16, NRSV

The entire parable recorded in Luke 20:9-16 focuses on the matter of delegated authority. God did not come personally to gather His due after He had rented the vineyard to the tenants. Three times He sent His servants, and the fourth time He sent His own Son. These all were His delegates. He wanted to see if the tenants would be subject to His delegated authorities. He could have come and collected, Himself, but He sent delegates instead.

In God's view, those who reject His servants reject Him. It is impossible for us to hearken to God's Word and not to the words of His delegates. If we are subject to God's authority, then we must also be subject to His delegated authority. Other than in Acts 9:4-15, which illustrates the direct authority of the Lord, the rest of the Bible demonstrates the authority He has delegated. It does not require humility to be obedient to God's direct authority, but it does demand humbleness and broken-ness to be subject to delegated authority.

Unless one sets aside the flesh completely, he is not able to receive and to hearken to delegated authority. May we realize that instead of coming Himself, He sends His delegates to collect His due. What, then, should be our attitude toward God? Shall we wait until God Himself comes? Remember that when He appears He will come to judge, not to collect!

The Lord showed Paul how he had kicked against the goads when he had resisted the Lord. Once Paul saw the light and saw authority, however, he asked, "What shall I do, Lord?" By this action he put himself under the direct authority of the Lord. Nevertheless, the Lord immediately shifted Paul to His delegated authority. "Rise, and enter into the city, and it shall be told thee what thou must do" (Acts 9:6).

From here on Paul recognized authority. He did not consider himself so exceptional that he would only listen if the Lord Himself told him what to do. During their very first encounter the Lord put Paul under His delegated authority.

How about us? Since we have believed in the Lord, how much have we been subject to delegated authority? To how many delegated authorities have we been submissive?

—*The Normal Christian Life*

QUESTIONS TO CONSIDER

1. Who has God placed in authority over you?
2. How do you feel about submitting to the authority figures in your life?

A PRAYERFUL RESPONSE

Lord, I will submit to those in authority over me. Amen.

PART THREE

Filled With His Power

Would you be free from the burden of sin?
There's power in the blood, power in the blood;
Would you o'er evil a victory win?
There's wonderful power in the blood.

There is power, power, wonder-working power
In the blood of the Lamb.
There is power, power, wonder working power
In the precious blood of the Lamb.

"THERE IS POWER IN THE BLOOD"
BY LEWIS E. JONES

WATCHMAN NEE'S INSIGHT
The Spirit of Christ fills us with power for living.

The Life of God

THOUGHT FOR TODAY
The life of God in us creates both death and resurrection.

WISDOM FROM SCRIPTURE
Teach me, O LORD, to follow your decrees; then I will keep them to the end.

Give me understanding, and I will keep your law and obey it with all my heart.

Direct me in the path of your commands, for there I find delight.

Turn my heart toward your statutes and not toward selfish gain.

Turn my eyes away from worthless things; preserve my life according to your word.

Fulfill your promise to your servant, so that you may be feared.

Take away the disgrace I dread, for your laws are good.

How I long for your precepts! Preserve my life in your righteousness.

PSALM 119:33-40, NIV

INSIGHTS FROM WATCHMAN NEE
If we allow the life of God to operate in us by obeying it, this will naturally result in growth and expansion. By letting this life work unceasingly within us—even in our conscience, our mind, our will, and our emotion—it will take away all unwanted things

and deposit in us the riches that come from God.

This process of subtracting a little and adding a little goes on continually in us. The more the subtraction, the more the addition. What is subtracted is Adam, what is added is Christ. What is subtracted is the old, what is added is the new. What is subtracted is the dead, what is added is the living. Undergoing subtraction and addition, little by little, our life continues to grow.

When the life of God operates in us there will be two effects: one is the effect of death, the other is the effect of resurrection. The effect of death takes away the sickness, whereas the effect of resurrection restores health. The first element of the Lord's cross is death; its second element is resurrection. We are told in Romans 6 that these two are the strongest and most effective elements of the life of Christ.

Now what is the cross? It is this, that when your heart is touched by God, you offer yourself into God's hand in order that His life may operate in you. And as it operates, there is an element that puts you to death. This effect of death takes away from you all that is undesired—that which rebels against God, that which is contrary to life, and that which is contradictory to the Holy Spirit. Meanwhile, there is also a living element, which causes you to live. The effect of this life is to enable you to live out all the riches of the Godhead, and so filling you with light, joy and peace.

This is how both the death and life of Christ work in you to deliver you from sin—from all that God hates and condemns—and at the same time it gives you freshness, light, joy and peace. As goes the subtracted, so comes the added. The life of God will operate and revolve around until little by little something is removed and something is left. As God's life operates, you will both die a little and come alive a little. It operates without ceasing, taking away more of the undesired and leaving behind more of the desired. The more the dead is removed, the more that living is increased. May we follow the operation of God's life, letting it pass through all our inward parts and work without obstacle that it may always have something to take away and something to add on.

The Bible declares that "the king's heart is in the hand of Jehovah as the water courses: he turneth it whithersoever he will" (Prv 21:1). If only we are willing to put our heart in God's hand, He is able to turn us around. Should we pray in this manner—"incline my heart unto thy testimonies, and not to covetousness" (Ps 119:36)—God will bring about the turning around of the heart.

When you begin, a truly saved person, your heart has been renewed. Even if you should ever become cold and turn inside, you know inwardly what has transpired. God has mercy upon you, and His life operates in you, until one day you pray audibly or silently: "O God, incline my heart toward You!" Given this little ground, His life operates further, even intensified, until your heart rises up and turns to God.

—*The Better Covenant*

QUESTIONS TO CONSIDER

1. What prompts you to incline your heart toward God?
2. What "subtraction" and "addition" does your heart need?

A PRAYERFUL RESPONSE

Lord, subtract the spiritually dead parts of me and replace them with Your life. Amen.

Living in the Spirit

THOUGHT FOR TODAY
Only the Holy Spirit creates spiritual reality.

WISDOM FROM SCRIPTURE
"Sir," the woman said, "I can see that you are a prophet.

"Our fathers worshiped on this mountain, but you Jews claim that the place where we must worship is in Jerusalem."

Jesus declared, "Believe me, woman, a time is coming when you will worship the Father neither on this mountain nor in Jerusalem.

"You Samaritans worship what you do not know; we worship what we do know, for salvation is from the Jews.

"Yet a time is coming and has now come when the true worshipers will worship the Father in spirit and truth, for they are the kind of worshipers the Father seeks.

"God is spirit, and his worshipers must worship in spirit and in truth."

JOHN 4:19-24, NIV

INSIGHTS FROM WATCHMAN NEE
One thing God's people should take note of is that every spiritual matter has its reality before God. If what we have touched is mere appearance and not reality, we shall find that it is of no spiritual value whatsoever.

What, then, is spiritual reality? The reality of a spiritual thing is something spiritual, not material. Although spiritual reality is often expressed in words, those words, however many, are not the reality. Although spiritual reality needs to be disclosed in our lives, the set formalities of our lives are not reality. Although spiritual reality must be manifested in conduct, human-manufactured pretension is not reality.

What is spiritual reality? "God is Spirit, and they that worship him," says the Lord, "must worship in spirit and truth." The word *truth* means "trueness" or "reality." The same applies to the following words: "Howbeit, when he, the Spirit of truth, is come, he shall guide you into all the truth." And it is the Spirit that beareth witness, because the Spirit is the truth.

These all reveal that God is Spirit, therefore all that is related to God is in the Spirit. The Spirit of truth is the Spirit of reality. For this reason, spiritual reality must be in the Spirit. It is that which transcends man and matter. Only what is in the Holy Spirit is spiritually real, because all spiritual things are nurtured in the Holy Spirit. Once anything is outside the Holy Spirit, it turns into letters and forms that are dead. Spiritual things are real, living and full of life only when they are in the Holy Spirit.

It is the Holy Spirit who guides us into all reality. Whatever may be entered into without the guidance of the Holy Spirit is definitely not spiritual reality. All that one can obtain merely by listening or thinking or being emotionally involved, is not spiritual reality. We must remember that the Holy Spirit is the Executor of all spiritual matters. What God does today is done in the Holy Spirit. Only what the Holy Spirit does is truly real.

Spiritual progress is not a question of attaining to some abstract standard, not a question of pressing through to some far-off goal; it is wholly a question of seeing God's standard.

Spiritual progress comes by finding out what you really are, not trying to be who you hope to be. You will never reach that goal, however earnestly you strive.

It is when you see that you are dead that you die; it is when you see that you are risen that you rise; it is when you see that you are holy that you become holy. It is seeing the goal that determines the pathway to the goal. The goal is revealed by inward seeing, not by desiring or by working. There is only one possibility of spiritual progress, and that is by discovering God's facts. Our great need is to see the truth as God sees it—the truth concerning Christ, the truth concerning ourselves in Christ, and the truth concerning the Church, the Body of Christ.

—The Finest of the Wheat, Volume 1

QUESTIONS TO CONSIDER

1. How would you describe your current understanding of spiritual reality?
2. How could better discernment of spiritual reality help you grow as a Christian?

A PRAYERFUL RESPONSE

Lord, I believe Your words are the only spiritual reality. Amen.

DAY 22

The Power of Pressure

THOUGHT FOR TODAY
Difficult circumstances increase our reliance on God.

WISDOM FROM SCRIPTURE
We do not want you to be uninformed, brothers, about the hardships we suffered in the province of Asia. We were under great pressure, far beyond our ability to endure, so that we despaired even of life.

Indeed, in our hearts we felt the sentence of death. But this happened that we might not rely on ourselves but on God, who raises the dead.

He has delivered us from such a deadly peril, and he will deliver us. On him we have set our hope that he will continue to deliver us.

2 CORINTHIANS 1:8-10, NIV

INSIGHTS FROM WATCHMAN NEE
God allows believers to pass through the pressure of circumstances so that they may live well before Him. Frequently, adverse situations arise in believers' circumstances. Some are troubled by their home folks; others are disturbed by friends. Some may incur business losses; others may be pushed around by colleagues. Some may be opposed or misunderstood by people; others may have financial difficulties. Why do all these things come upon them?

Many believers ordinarily do not realize how precious is the regenerated life they have received. Though they are born again, they nonetheless are ignorant of the pricelessness of their regenerated life. But once they come under pressure, they begin to appreciate their regenerated life because the new life that God gave to them enables them to overcome in all circumstances. All these external pressures can prove the reality of this regenerated life and of its power. The Lord purposely places us in adverse circumstances in order to remind us that without His life we cannot stand. The power of His life is made manifest through outside pressure.

If, for example, your heart is being pierced by a certain affair that causes you to weep in secret, and you acknowledge that you are totally helpless and beyond any comfort, you will gain complete victory if at that moment you cast yourself upon God. You will be amazed at the greatness of the power which gives you victory. This external pressure causes you to spontaneously trust God, thus enabling you in turn to manifest the reality and the power of the Lord's life.

Naturally, for those who have not believed in the Lord and do not possess this regenerated life, they will no doubt be crushed under the heavy pressure of such agonizing circumstances. A Christian, however, is regenerated; and so he has a life within him which is stronger than any outside pressure. When he is pressed, then does he overcome, since the pressure of circumstances simply substantiates the regenerated life within him.

I once read a pamphlet entitled, "Be a Gas Machine." It told the story of a particular person. In the American city of Pittsburgh, the entire community at that time was using gas lamps. The owner of the gas company was a Christian. One time he began to encounter many adverse circumstances. His clients frequently accused him of things having no connection with him at all. People doing business with him opposed him and refused to give him the normal courtesies due him. So he prayed to God, asking the Lord to grant him power to overcome all these difficulties. But after he had thus prayed, his situation only grew worse.

One day an employee came to tell him that all the machines in the factory had ceased functioning. No one knew why or could find out which part had broken down. Consequently, the owner himself had to go and inspect the situation. In his examination, he found out that the machinery was all intact except that a small valve in the boiler was broken. Without any pressure, whatever steam had been produced could still not be utilized, thus signifying that none of the machines would operate.

It was at that moment that he heard a still, small voice saying to him, "You should be a gas machine." Later on he testified that this gas machinery had spoken to him as the ass had spoke to Balaam in the olden days. Praise and thank God. He also attested to the fact that because the valve was broken, there was no pressure; and without pressure, the lamps of the entire city could give no light. Yet the presence of pressure would cause the lamps of the city to shine. So he should not resist pressure in his life. He ought instead to be a gas machine.

Do let us see that the power of a person's life cannot exceed the pressure he receives.

—*From Faith to Faith*

QUESTIONS TO CONSIDER

1. What past situations increased your reliance on God?
2. What circumstances do you need to turn over to God's care?

A PRAYERFUL RESPONSE

Lord, thank You for using circumstances for my good and Your glory. Amen.

Why Do We Pray?

THOUGHT FOR TODAY

Prayer ushers in God's will for us.

WISDOM FROM SCRIPTURE

"And when you pray, do not be like the hypocrites, for they love to pray standing in the synagogues and on the street corners to be seen by men. I tell you the truth, they have received their reward in full.

"But when you pray, go into your room, close the door and pray to your Father, who is unseen. Then your Father, who sees what is done in secret, will reward you.

"And when you pray, do not keep on babbling like pagans, for they think they will be heard because of their many words.

"Do not be like them, for your Father knows what you need before you ask him.

"This, then, is how you should pray: 'Our Father in heaven, hallowed be your name, your kingdom come, your will be done on earth as it is in heaven.

"'Give us today our daily bread.

"'Forgive us our debts, as we also have forgiven our debtors.

"'And lead us not into temptation, but deliver us from the evil one.'"

MATTHEW 6:5-13, NIV

INSIGHTS FROM WATCHMAN NEE

A servant of the Lord has well said: Prayer is the rail for God's work. Indeed, prayer is to God's will as rails are to a train. The locomotive is full of power: it is capable of running a thousand miles a day. But if there are no rails, it cannot move forward a single inch. If it dares to move without them, it will soon sink into the earth. It may be able to travel great distances, yet it cannot go to any place where no rails have been laid.

And such is the relationship between prayer and God's work. I do not believe it necessary to explain in detail, for I trust everyone can recognize the meaning of this parable. Without any doubt God is almighty and He works mightily, but He will not and cannot work if you and I do not labor together with Him in prayer, prepare the way for His will, and pray "with all prayer and supplication" (Eph 6:18) to grant Him the maneuverability to so work.

Many are the things which God wills to do and would like to do, but His hands are bound because His children do not sympathize with Him and have not prayed so as to prepare ways for Him. Let me say to all who have wholly given themselves to God: Do examine yourselves and see if in this respect you have limited Him day after day.

Hence our most important work is to prepare the way of the Lord. There is no other work which can be compared with this work. With God there are many "possibilities," but these will turn into "impossibilities" if believers do not open up ways for Him. In view of this, our prayers in one mind with God must be greatly increased. May we pray exhaustively—that is to say, may we pray through in all directions—so that God's will may prosper at all points. Though our activities among men are important, our working together with the Lord by prayers offered up before Him is much more important.

Prayer is not an attempt to restore heaven's heart. It is a most erroneous concept to hold that God being hard, we therefore need to engage in combat against Him in prayer as to subjugate Him and thereby cause Him to alter His decision. Whatever prayer is not according to God's will is utterly void. Let us see that we strive before God as in conflict, only because His will is being blocked by either men or the devil, and so we greatly desire Him to execute His will in order that His own determinate will may not suffer because of opposition.

But so desiring after God's determinate will and praying—yea, even striving—against all that oppose His will, we prepare the way for Him to carry out His determinate will without permitting that which comes out of man or of the devil temporarily to prevail. True, we seem to be striving against God; yet such striving is not aimed against God as though to compel Him to change His will to suit our pleasure, but it is against all that is opposed to God, so that He may fulfill His will. In view of this, let us see that we are unable to pray as fellow workers of God unless we really know what His will is.

Oh, let us see that prayer in sympathy with God is more vital than any other thing! For God can only work in matters for which His children have shown sympathy. He refuses to work in areas where there are no prayers and where His people's will is not united with His will. Prayer with joined wills is real prayer. The highest motive of prayer is not in having it answered. It is to join man's will with God's so that He may work. Sometimes we may ask incorrectly and thus our prayer goes unanswered; yet if our will is joined with God's, He will still gain, for through our sympathy He is still able to work out His will.

—*Let Us Pray*

QUESTIONS TO CONSIDER

1 In prayer, do you usually seek to change God's mind or do
you seek God's will? Why?

2. How can you seek God's will as you pray?

A PRAYERFUL RESPONSE

Lord, please reveal Your will to me as I pray today. Amen.

Walking in God's Will

THOUGHT FOR TODAY

God's perfect will is greater than His permissive will.

WISDOM FROM SCRIPTURE

So Balaam got up in the morning, saddled his donkey, and went with the officials of Moab.

God's anger was kindled because he was going, and the angel of the Lord took his stand in the road as his adversary. Now he was riding on the donkey, and his two servants were with him.

The donkey saw the angel of the Lord standing in the road, with a drawn sword in his hand; so the donkey turned off the road, and went into the field; and Balaam struck the donkey, to turn it back onto the road.

Then the angel of the Lord stood in a narrow path between the vineyards, with a wall on either side.

When the donkey saw the angel of the Lord, it scraped against the wall, and scraped Balaam's foot against the wall; so he struck it again.

Then the angel of the Lord went ahead, and stood in a narrow place, where there was no way to turn either to the right or to the left.

When the donkey saw the angel of the Lord, it lay down under Balaam and Balaam's anger was kindled, and he struck the donkey with his staff.

Then the Lord opened the mouth of the donkey, and it said

to Balaam, "What have I done to you, that you have struck me these three times?"

Balaam said to the donkey, "Because you have made a fool of me! I wish I had a sword in my hand! I would kill you right now!"

But the donkey said to Balaam, "Am I not your donkey, which you have ridden all your life to this day? Have I been in the habit of treating you this way?" And he said, "No."

Then the Lord opened the eyes of Balaam, and he saw the angel of the Lord standing in the road, with his drawn sword in his hand; and he bowed down, falling on his face.

The angel of the Lord said to him, "Why have you struck your donkey these three times? I have come out as an adversary because your way is perverse before me.

"The donkey saw me, and turned away from me these three times. If it had not turned away from me, surely just now I would have killed you and let it live."

Then Balaam said to the angel of the Lord, "I have sinned, for I did not know that you were standing in the road to oppose me. Now therefore, if it is displeasing to you, I will return home."

NUMBERS 22:21-34, NRSV

INSIGHTS FROM WATCHMAN NEE

We must walk in the direct will of God and not in His permissive will. The direct will of God is that original mind in the heart of God that He commands us (or guides us) to follow. The permissive will of God, on the other hand, is that which He permits us to do after our (often persistent) entreaties.

Let us take the following as an example: The parents see the need one day of an outing for their children. So they take them out for a day. Days later, their children wish to take another trip because they loved the beautiful scenery they saw the first time. The parents, however, do not see such a need. Yet, due to their children's persistent request and their failure to persuade the children otherwise, the parents finally permit them to go out a second time. Here we see that the first outing is the direct will of parents, whereas the second outing is their permissive will. Many believers come to God asking—and even insistently so— for permission to do a certain thing, instead of coming to God inquiring if the thing in question is according to His will. This is truly lamentable!

A review of an incident recorded in the Old Testament will help us understand this matter better. In Numbers 22 we learn that the Moabite king, Balak, had sent emissaries to the prophet Balaam inviting him to come and curse the children of Israel. He promised to give the prophet great rewards, which moved the latter's heart (see Jude 11; 2 Pt 2:15). Balaam indeed wanted to go, but having the fear of God in him, he felt he must ask Jehovah first before any decision was made. "And God said unto Balaam, Thou shalt not go with them; thou shalt not curse the people; for they are blessed" (Nm 22:12). This was unquestionably God's direct will.

Now after receiving this word from the Lord, Balaam ought to have given up any thought of going. But he told the princes of Balak, "Get you into your land; for Jehovah refuseth to give me leave to go with you" (verse 13). How reluctant in sound is the word "refuse" that comes from the mouth of the prophet. It was as though Balaam had said to them, "It is not because I would not wish to go, but because the Lord does not allow me to go." Whereupon Balak sent princes again to Balaam and promised to promote the latter into great honor. So Balaam came to God once more to ask.

How strange, Balaam! Did not God already tell you on your first approach to Him what His mind and will is? Why do you come to ask the Lord again? Do you think because you are moved by great honor that God, too, will be so moved? Do you think His will is subject to change? Do you not know that He is the same yesterday, today and forever?

Let us clearly understand here that if Balaam had really wanted to do God's will, he should have frankly told these men on their second visit to him: "God already plainly told me last time that I should not go. So, please return. I will never go." But his greediness so overcame him that he came and entreated Jehovah a second time. Then God said to Balaam: "Rise up, go with them" (verse 20). What the Lord meant by His words was: "Since I am not able to restrain you, you may simply go," which the prophet did and went his way.

Now many today do not understand why the angel of Jehovah later came to block Balaam's way to kill him, they not realizing that the way of Balaam was crooked before the Lord (see again 2 Pt 2:15, 16; Num 22:32b). The same is true in the experience of many Christians today in their walk. They know already in their hearts that the Lord does not want them to do certain things, yet they still love to do them. And whenever opportunities come, therefore, they continue to annoy God by asking. Even though they may not do these things for a time, their hearts have nonetheless already departed from God. And if they eventually do get the Lord's permission, who can question the discipline of the Lord which—as in the case of Balaam with the angel of Jehovah—may follow? For this reason, we must get the Lord's "best," not His "second best." Whoever has a heart that is estranged from God, and yet seeks the Lord's will as a cover, will be disciplined.

—*Take Heed*

QUESTIONS TO CONSIDER
1. How can you tell the difference between God's perfect and permissive will?
2. Which is easier to choose? Why?

A PRAYERFUL RESPONSE
Lord, I choose to seek Your perfect will for my life. Amen.

Wondrous Things Are Done

THOUGHT FOR TODAY

Nothing is impossible or too extraordinary for God.

WISDOM FROM SCRIPTURE

For he will deliver the needy who cry out, the afflicted who have no one to help.

He will take pity on the weak and the needy and save the needy from death.

He will rescue them from oppression and violence, for precious is their blood in his sight.

Long may he live! May gold from Sheba be given him. May people ever pray for him and bless him all day long.

Let grain abound throughout the land; on the tops of the hills may it sway. Let its fruit flourish like Lebanon; let it thrive like the grass of the field.

May his name endure forever; may it continue as long as the sun. All nations will be blessed through him, and they will call him blessed.

Praise be to the Lord God, the God of Israel, who alone does marvelous deeds.

PSALM 72:12-18, NIV

"And these signs will accompany those who believe: In my name they will drive out demons; they will speak in new tongues; they will pick up snakes with their hands; and when they drink deadly poison, it will not hurt them at all; they will place their hands on sick people, and they will get well."

MARK 16:17-18, NIV

Let us well remember one spiritual principle: that faith is most natural and effortless. Some Christians do not understand much about faith, so having their prayers answered seems to require much labor. Each time they try to obtain God's answer, they have to apply such a heavy dose of faith that they almost cry out, "I am here believing! I am here believing!" Although their prayers may be heard, they have believed to the point of exhaustion. After having enough experience and having learned more, they pray, they believe, and God hears them, but they now have no need to exert so much effort as before. They will pray quite naturally, and God will answer them quite naturally. Formerly, their faith was so forced that it nearly broke their heart. They wanted to believe but they could not believe. They believed till they were exhausted in their faith. Now their faith is something very natural; it is spontaneous faith.

Faith is spontaneous, and wondrous works are natural. No one who works wonders fancies he is working wonders. To the one who truly believes in God, wondrous works are quite common. Only those who are far away from God deem them extraordinary. All who live before God, and close to Him, consider wondrous works to be something ordinary.

At one time or another we must have all read the story of the children of Israel crossing the Red Sea. The first time we read it, we must have been amazed at the multitudes of people who crossed the Red Sea. Yet the Bible never recorded anything like shoutings by the people on this side of the Red Sea, saying, "How marvelous, the waters are divided!" or "Look, what a wonder this is!" No, they simply composed a song and sang only after they landed on the other side of the sea. As they looked back, they realized what a great wonder it was. It is the same with the believers today. When the Lord works wonders in their lives, they have no idea that these are wondrous works. Only when they look back do they comprehend the greatness of God's works.

Recall, if you will, how many times God has healed your sickness. At those times, did you really think great things had happened? Many times you have encountered problems which were solved through God's grace, but at those moments did you understand God as working wonders? No, not until you looked back did you realize what great things had happened. Even this looking back is natural, and not deliberate.

Some people, viewing these verses from the human side, misconclude the words in Mark 16:17-18 to signify the things mentioned there to be quite extraordinary. Yet as we think upon God, we will not at all be surprised. Compared to the crossing of the Red Sea by the children of Israel, these other things in Mark are quite insignificant. The words in Mark do not mean that a believer can drink deadly things every day without dying. No, if anyone should drink deadly things deliberately, he will surely die.

On the contrary, the Mark passage simply suggests our knowing God and His power: we acknowledge that there is nothing He cannot do. For wonders do not come by believing with great effort; they are the manifestations of God's mighty power. He is the God who works wonders. Whenever He works, wonders are performed. And furthermore, you and I will have no sense that doing wondrous works is difficult at all. The problem today lies in viewing these wonders from a great distance, divorced from a true consideration of God, and thus wonders, within that kind of context, cannot help but become something very extraordinary. To those who are near to God, however, wonders are something quite commonplace in the house of God.

—*The Spirit of the Gospel*

QUESTIONS TO CONSIDER

1. What wondrous things has God accomplished in your life?
2. Did you see them as extraordinary at the time, or only in looking back?

A PRAYERFUL RESPONSE

Lord, I believe You will work wondrous miracles in my life. Amen.

DAY 26

Resist the Devil

Fear is Satan's calling card.

Finally, be strong in the Lord and in his mighty power.

Put on the full armor of God so that you can take your stand against the devil's schemes.

For our struggle is not against flesh and blood, but against the rulers, against the authorities, against the powers of this dark world and against the spiritual forces of evil in the heavenly realms.

Therefore put on the full armor of God, so that when the day of evil comes, you may be able to stand your ground, and after you have done everything, to stand.

Stand firm then, with the belt of truth buckled around your waist, with the breastplate of righteousness in place, and with your feet fitted with the readiness that comes from the gospel of peace.

In addition to all this, take up the shield of faith, with which you can extinguish all the flaming arrows of the evil one.

Take the helmet of salvation and the sword of the Spirit, which is the word of God.

Be self-controlled and alert. Your enemy the devil prowls around like a roaring lion looking for someone to devour.

Resist him, standing firm in the faith, because you know that your brothers throughout the world are undergoing the same kind of sufferings.

EPHESIANS 6:10-17; 1 PETER 5:8-9, NIV

Whenever Satan works against God's children, he must first secure some ground in them. Ephesians exhorts us, "Neither give place to the devil" (4:27). Without a foothold, Satan cannot operate. Hence, his first tempting of us will be in order to secure a ground; his next will be an assault on us from the ground he has already secured. Our victory lies in not giving him any ground from the very beginning. One very large ground, perhaps the very largest, that he seeks is fear. Satan's characteristically customary work is to instill fear in the mind of God's children, a foreboding that something is going to happen.

Let us note the words of Job: "For the thing which I fear cometh upon me, and that which I am afraid of cometh unto me" (3:25). What this verse reveals to us is of tremendous significance. Before these terrible things happened to him, Job already had some apprehension. He was fearful lest his children would die; he was afraid that he might lose all his property. Satan's first job is to plant this fear in man. If the fear is accepted, things will soon happen; if it is rejected, nothing will come of it. Satan has to obtain one's consent before he can operate. If this consent is withheld, he cannot work, for man is created with a free will. Without man's consent, Satan can neither tempt him to sin nor attack him at will. So, in the case of Job, Satan first implanted a tiny little thought of fear in Job. Having once accepted the thought, it made Job tremble.

"Fear is Satan's calling card," said Miss Margaret E. Barber. And whenever you accept his calling card, you receive a visit from him. If you reject his calling card, you drive him away. Fear him, and he comes; fear not, and he is kept away.

Therefore, refuse to be afraid! Perhaps one will eventually kill himself if he is obsessed by the thought of cutting his throat while shaving. How often men have thoughts of fear in them, fearful lest this or that thing happen. This is especially true of nervous people. But remember, these thoughts come from Satan and must be resisted.

To the question of what is meant by resistance, an elderly person once replied, "To resist means to say, 'Thank you, but I do not want it,' when something is offered to you." Whatever is offered you, you always answer "No, thanks!" Though Satan may present you with this or that thing, your reaction is a simple refusal. Such an attitude is enough; it is all that is needed to defeat his purpose. Let us learn this lesson today: resist every thought of fear. Fear not, for fear will bring to you the very thing you are afraid of. May I remind you that no child of God should be fearful of Satan because Satan cannot overcome us. Although he is quite powerful, we have in us One who is greater than he. This is an unchangeable fact, "because greater is he that is in you than he that is in the world" (1 Jn 4:4). Therefore, never accept fear. He who accepts fear is a fool. Has not the Bible clearly taught that, by resisting Satan, he will flee? What place does he have in us except to retreat!

The second condition of resistance is to know the truth. "Ye shall know the truth, and the truth shall make you free" (Jn 8:32).

What is truth? Truth is the reality of a thing. When Satan tempts or frightens or attacks people, he always comes in stealthily. He never lets you know he is there. He will not proclaim aloud that he has arrived, for that would arouse your suspicion. He lies, he counterfeits. He never does anything in the light. But if you know what the reality of the thing is, it will set you free. In other words, if you know something is of Satan, you are freed. The difficulty for many children of God is their unawareness of the enemy. They may say with their mouths that it is Satan's attack, yet they do not sense it deep down in their spirits. Though their lips pronounce it to be the work of Satan, their spirits are not as clear. But the day they see the truth, really knowing that this is Satan's work, they are instantly set free.

The power of Satan lies in his deception. If he cannot deceive, he loses his power. Hence, seeing makes resistance easy. When you are surrounded with perils in your environment, you cannot overcome if you only feel that these may be satanic attacks. You need to know for sure that these are of Satan, and then it is easy for you to withstand. To deal with Satan takes more than opposing, for it is difficult to fight against his falsehoods. But when you meet him, you need to recognize him as such; then resist, and he will flee from you.

—*Love One Another*

QUESTIONS TO CONSIDER

1. Do you have seeds of fear in your life? If so, what are they?
2. How can you stand against the lies of Satan?

A PRAYERFUL RESPONSE

Lord, thank You for the strength to say "no, thank you" to Satan. Amen.

To Know Him

THOUGHT FOR TODAY

God desires that we know Him and His calling for us.

WISDOM FROM SCRIPTURE

For this reason, ever since I heard about your faith in the Lord Jesus and your love for all the saints,

I have not stopped giving thanks for you, remembering you in my prayers.

I keep asking that the God of our Lord Jesus Christ, the glorious Father, may give you the Spirit of wisdom and revelation, so that you may know him better.

I pray also that the eyes of your heart may be enlightened in order that you may know the hope to which he has called you, the riches of his glorious inheritance in the saints, and his incomparably great power for us who believe. That power is like the working of his mighty strength, which he exerted in Christ when he raised him from the dead and seated him at his right hand in the heavenly realms, far above all rule and authority, power and dominion, and every title that can be given, not only in the present age but also in the one to come.

And God placed all things under his feet and appointed him to be head over everything for the church, which is his body, the fullness of him who fills everything in every way.

EPHESIANS 1:15-23, NIV

As we begin to know God, His purpose ordained in eternity, and His work throughout the ages, we shall increasingly realize how many-sided, lofty and special are the insights which God reveals to us in Paul's Letter to the Ephesians. We cannot fail to notice this one thing, that in this letter God causes Paul to record the fact that he prays two prayers: the one prayer as mentioned in chapter 1, and the other prayer that is mentioned in chapter 3.

The first prayer is foundational, whereas the second prayer is for building up. In the first chapter, Paul's prayer is for us to know our relationship with the Lord, while in the third chapter his prayer is for us to know our relationship with the church, as well as that with the Lord. We will at present only concentrate on the prayer found in the first chapter of Ephesians.

Paul begins his prayer with these words: "that the God of our Lord Jesus Christ, the Father of glory, may give unto you a spirit of wisdom and revelation." Why does he long for the Ephesian believers to have the spirit of wisdom and revelation? Quite simply, that they may know the following three things:

(1) "The knowledge of him" (verse 17). This is knowing God Himself.

(2) "That ye may know what is the hope of his calling, what is the riches of the glory of his inheritance in the saints" (verse 18). This points to the eternal plan of God and its fulfillment. The gracious calling of God is a calling of us to be His sons, and these sons shall be His inheritance. The call of God was preordained before the foundation of the world, whereas the

riches of the glory of His inheritance in the saints will be realized in the eternity to come. In eternity past, God has a will; and in eternity to come He will have a possession. The putting together of these two facts reveals the eternal purpose and plan of God. So that what Paul wants us to know is God's eternal plan.

And (3) "What the exceeding greatness of his power to usward who believe" (verse 19). This statement shows us what power God will use today to achieve His purpose and to accomplish His plan. Hence it deals especially with our relationship to Him today, and also our relationship to His purpose in eternity.

These things we need to consider and to have revelation about before God.

—The Spirit of Wisdom and Revelation

QUESTIONS TO CONSIDER

1. How well do you know God?
2. What is your understanding of His calling for your life?

A PRAYERFUL RESPONSE

Lord, I ask for the wisdom to know You and Your calling for me. Amen.

An Offering to God

THOUGHT FOR TODAY

We are to offer ourselves as living sacrifices to God.

WISDOM FROM SCRIPTURE

He is to lay his hand on the head of the burnt offering, and it will be accepted on his behalf to make atonement for him.

He is to lay his hand on the head of his offering and slaughter it at the entrance to the Tent of Meeting. Then Aaron's sons the priests shall sprinkle the blood against the altar on all sides.

He is to lay his hand on the head of his offering and slaughter it in front of the Tent of Meeting. Then Aaron's sons shall sprinkle its blood against the altar on all sides.

He is to lay his hand on its head and slaughter it in front of the Tent of Meeting. Then Aaron's sons shall sprinkle its blood against the altar on all sides.

He is to present the bull at the entrance to the Tent of Meeting before the Lord. He is to lay his hand on its head and slaughter it before the Lord.

The elders of the community are to lay their hands on the bull's head before the Lord, and the bull shall be slaughtered before the Lord.

He is to lay his hand on the goat's head and slaughter it at the place where the burnt offering is slaughtered before the Lord. It is a sin offering.

He is to lay his hand on the head of the sin offering and

slaughter it at the place of the burnt offering.

He is to lay his hand on its head and slaughter it for a sin offering at the place where the burnt offering is slaughtered.

LEVITICUS 1:4; 3:2, 8, 13; 4:4, 15, 24, 29, 33, NIV

INSIGHTS FROM WATCHMAN NEE

In the Old Testament we find that the laying on of hands has a double significance. It is mentioned most frequently in Leviticus, chapters 1, 3, and 4, so we will look there to find its first meaning.

The laying on of my hand on the head of the sacrifice in Leviticus 1 signifies that I am identified with the sacrifice and the sacrifice with me. Why do I not offer myself to God, but offer a bullock instead? "For every beast of the forest is mine, and the cattle upon a thousand hills" (Ps 50:10), says the Lord. What is the use of bringing cattle or sheep to Him? God does not lack a bullock or a lamb. He wants people to offer themselves.

But what would happen if I actually came to the altar and offered myself? I would be doing the same things as the Gentiles did, as those who worshiped Moloch. In the Old Testament, there were people who served Moloch. Instead of offering cattle and sheep, they sacrificed their own sons and daughters on the altar to their god. Does our God desire only cattle or sheep? If we offer ourselves to God, how is our God different from Moloch? He is different in that Moloch demanded the blood of our sons and daughters, but our God requires us to offer ourselves. His charge is even more severe than that of Moloch.

It is true that God's demand is more strict, but He shows us a way whereby we may sacrifice and yet not be burned. How? I bring a bullock or a lamb to the Lord. I lay my hand upon the head of the sacrifice. Whether I pray audibly or silently, my prayer is: This is me. I myself should be on the altar and be consumed by fire. I myself ought to be sacrificed, and would indeed gladly offer myself to You. I should offer myself to be a burnt-offering, a sweet savor unto You. Lord, I now bring this bullock with me, and upon its head I lay my hand. By doing this, Lord, it signifies that this bullock is me, and I am this bullock. When I ask the priest to slay it, it is as if I am slain. When the blood of the bullock flows, my blood flows. When the priest sets the sacrifice on the altar, he has put me on the altar. I have laid my hand on it, so it is me.

Is not the same principle of identification illustrated in baptism? When I step into the water, I say this is my grave, for the Lord has buried me in it. I take the water as my grave. Likewise, as I lay my hand on the head of the bullock, I take the bullock as myself. When I offer it to God, I offer myself. The bullock stands for me.

Hence, the first meaning of the laying on of hands is identification. This is its prime significance in the Old Testament. I am identified with the sacrifice, and it is me. Today both the sacrifice and I stand in the same position. When it is brought to God, I am brought to God.

There is a second significance to the laying on of hands in the Old Testament. In Genesis we see how Isaac laid his hands on his two sons, and how Jacob laid hands on his two grandsons, Ephraim and Manasseh (48:8-20). Jacob laid one hand on each of his grandsons and blessed them, so the laying on of hands becomes the impartation of blessing. With whatever blessing one is blessed, it shall come to pass.

In short, the significance of the laying on of hands is twofold: identification and impartation. These two may again be summed up by another word, communion. Through communion, we become identified; through communion, what one person has flows to another person.

—Assembling Together

QUESTIONS TO CONSIDER

1. How can you identify yourself as a living sacrifice?
2. What blessings can you impart to others?

A PRAYERFUL RESPONSE

Lord, I offer myself as a living sacrifice to You. Amen.

Rest Is Power

THOUGHT FOR TODAY

Resting in God's presence develops inward peace and power.

WISDOM FROM SCRIPTURE

This is what the Sovereign LORD, the Holy One of Israel, says: "In repentance and rest is your salvation, in quietness and trust is your strength, but you would have none of it."

ISAIAH 30:15, NIV

"Take my yoke upon you and learn from me, for I am gentle and humble in heart, and you will find rest for your souls."

MATTHEW 11:29, NIV

Do not be anxious about anything, but in everything, by prayer and petition, with thanksgiving, present your requests to God.

And the peace of God, which transcends all understanding, will guard your hearts and your minds in Christ Jesus.

PHILIPPIANS 4:6-7, NIV

INSIGHTS FROM WATCHMAN NEE

How can we live a peaceful and tranquil life? To answer this, we must see what the Lord says. He has not said that we should not work, nor has He said that we should work but half a day and spend the other half in spiritual things. He has not reprimanded Martha, saying that it is wrong for her to do many things. What the Lord reminds her of is that she should not allow herself to be anxious or troubled over many things. The Lord Jesus does not say she has done too much; He only mentions that she has thought too much, worried too much.

You may work from morning till night, but you should not be anxious and troubled all the day. Many people are not really too busy with outward things, though they are fairly busy inwardly. Some will be so anxious and busily occupied in their minds concerning the thing that is to happen five days later that they lose five nights rest in the process. Suppose it will take you but one hour to visit someone tomorrow, yet you dream about him for four hours at night. Then you are thinking too much. The Lord does not charge us not to do things; He only enjoins us not to be anxious and troubled while we do them. He does not say we have done too much; He merely says that we ought not be anxious and troubled.

This is the Christian life: that we ought to work diligently and not be lazy. It is right for us to labor hard, and it is not detrimental to be busy outwardly. Yet what is of vital importance is for us to be calm inwardly. Only one thing is allowed within—none other than Christ Himself. And this is what the Lord Jesus is showing us here. The Lord requires but one thing of us, which is, that in the midst of whatever circumstance, we are not to be touched by it. Physically we may toil hard and do many things, but inwardly there is no loosening up in the matter of our having this one thing. Outwardly we can be fully engrossed, yet inwardly we maintain constant fellowship with God.

Thank God, there is not only a Martha but there is also a Mary. Mary has chosen the good part, which is communion with the Lord. The Lord wants Martha to learn from her sister this matter of inner rest, not learn from her sister to do things. We can be Martha outwardly but never inwardly. Outwardly we may be Martha, but inwardly we must learn to be Mary in having perfect union with the Lord. Though busily engaged outwardly, there is calm fellowship with God inwardly. This is a most precious experience.

Take Brother Lawrence, for example. He had to prepare meals from morning till evening for many people. Now if this were our situation, we probably would be so busy as to lose our fellowship with God. Yet Brother Lawrence maintained such an inner communion with the Lord that outside things did not affect him at all. How truly he was one who knew the presence of the Lord. Outwardly he was busy all the time, yet inwardly he continually sat at God's feet. He had many things to do externally, but he was not perturbed in the least by these outside concerns.

This is the kind of precious life we all need. Every one of us can have such a life. This life finds its source in the depths of our being, not in our feeling or action. There in our depths is a constant fellowship with the Lord. We must always remember that God has not called us to be lazy and do nothing. He intends to dwell in us so that we are able to stand the hustle and bustle of life. We may be busily occupied from sunrise to sunset; yet however much we toil, nothing can cause us to lose the inward peace, nothing can deprive us of the river of rest. Externally we are busy, but internally there is rest.

Hence, never allow outside matters to touch you. You must resist the intrusion of outward things upon you. Whatever these external affairs may be, you must not let them penetrate to your depths. In you there is only one person, even Christ; within you there is only one exercise, to be near to Christ. If you permit any other thing to intrude, you will soon lose your inward peace.

—*Practical Issues of This Life*

QUESTIONS TO CONSIDER
1. In what circumstances do you worry most?
2. How can you better resist the temptation to be anxious?

A PRAYERFUL RESPONSE
Lord, I offer to You my worries about the work You have called me to do. Amen.

DAY 30

He That Overcometh

THOUGHT FOR TODAY
Through God's power, no situation is beyond recovery.

WISDOM FROM SCRIPTURE
"In that day you will no longer ask me anything. I tell you the truth, my Father will give you whatever you ask in my name.

"Until now you have not asked for anything in my name. Ask and you will receive, and your joy will be complete.

"Though I have been speaking figuratively, a time is coming when I will no longer use this kind of language but will tell you plainly about my Father.

"In that day you will ask in my name. I am not saying that I will ask the Father on your behalf.

"No, the Father himself loves you because you have loved me and have believed that I came from God.

"I came from the Father and entered the world; now I am leaving the world and going back to the Father."

Then Jesus' disciples said, "Now you are speaking clearly and without figures of speech.

"Now we can see that you know all things and that you do not even need to have anyone ask you questions. This makes us believe that you came from God."

"You believe at last!" Jesus answered.

"But a time is coming, and has come, when you will be scattered, each to his own home. You will leave me all alone. Yet I am not alone, for my Father is with me.

"I have told you these things, so that in me you may have peace. In this world you will have trouble. But take heart! I have overcome the world."

JOHN 16:23-33, NIV

INSIGHTS FROM WATCHMAN NEE

What is the meaning of an "overcomer"? To avoid misunderstanding, let it first be clear that these people are not Christians who are abnormally good. It is not that they are individually better than others, and therefore are destined to receive greater glory. Please remember, overcomers are simply normal Christians. All others have become, for the moment, subnormal.

In past eternity, God had a definite plan, a design which He has never abandoned. Overcomers are those who, having seen that design, have set themselves by God's grace to stand by it. They are not certain imaginary people who have gone further than Paul, or who take a different line from that revealed through Paul. They are, I repeat, no more than normal in God's eyes; they can claim no special credit.

Overcoming, in John's writings, does not mean simply the question of personal overcoming. It is not a matter of overcoming sin, which is better termed "deliverance," nor of personal holiness—the so-called "victorious life." The overcoming spoken of by John is the kind of overcoming that, in a given situation, lays claim to and holds that situation for God. In an hour when the Pauline message is rejected by so many, the Christian is tempted to say, "That is how things are. What can we do about it? We must just try to keep ourselves straight on certain lines, but we shall have to let some things pass as hopeless. They are beyond recovery. There is nothing we can do to improve them."

Beset by circumstances, real and hypothetical, which we simply do not know how to contend with, it is easy to resign ourselves to the view that our particular situation is beyond recovery. There are too many things in it to be adjusted, too many painful steps to be taken in the outworking. The thing is impossible.

It is in such an hour that overcomers reassert, by their life and testimony, that God is not a man that He should change. His standard, they affirm, has not altered, and He has still set Himself to have a heavenly city at the end, a heavenly Man today. What the whole church, as the church, ought to be doing but has left undone, they, representatively and for the church, are raised up by God to do. Standing true to the victorious heavenly Man, they hold their ground. That is the "overcoming" spoken of here in the Word.

John, in Revelation, shows the sphere of the overcomers. It is within the defeated church today. Those of importance to God are those who now, each in his own situation, lay claim to those situations for God. There is a part of God's plan that concerns each of us, just where we are, and for it He needs overcomers. I say again, there is no special goodness about them; their only distinction is that they are not abnormally bad! They abide by God's standard, that is all. But knowing the Christian life, the heavenly calling of the body, the warfare of the church, they are like a lever in God's hands to dislodge Satan from his throne. They prepare themselves on the church's behalf, and they fight for the church. They put out all their effort, not for their own sakes but for the sake of the body; and because they are ready. God sees the church prepared as a bride. They set the torch, as it were, to the fire, and what the overcomers inherit the whole church inherits.

—*What Shall This Man Do?*

QUESTIONS TO CONSIDER
1. What does "overcoming" mean to you?
2. How can you "hold your ground" in difficult circumstances?

A PRAYERFUL RESPONSE
Lord, I will seek Your strength to be an overcomer. Amen.

PART FOUR

Prepared for Service

Take my life and let it be
Consecrated, Lord, to Thee;
Take my moments and my days—
Let them flow in ceaseless praise,
Let them flow in ceaseless praise.

Take my will and make it Thine—
It shall be no longer mine;
Take my heart—it is thine own,
It shall be Thy royal throne,
It shall be Thy royal throne.

"TAKE MY LIFE AND LET IT BE"
BY FRANCIS RIDLEY HAVERGAL

WATCHMAN NEE'S INSIGHT
A consecrated life is a life in God's service.

What Is God's Work?

THOUGHT FOR TODAY

God gives us His power to accomplish His work.

WISDOM FROM SCRIPTURE

Paul, an apostle of Christ Jesus by the will of God, To the saints who are in Ephesus and are faithful in Christ Jesus: Grace to you and peace from God our Father and the Lord Jesus Christ.

Blessed be the God and Father of our Lord Jesus Christ, who has blessed us in Christ with every spiritual blessing in the heavenly places, just as he chose us in Christ before the foundation of the world to be holy and blameless before him in love.

He destined us for adoption as his children through Jesus Christ, according to the good pleasure of his will, to the praise of his glorious grace that he freely bestowed on us in the Beloved.

In him we have redemption through his blood, the forgiveness of our trespasses, according to the riches of his grace that he lavished on us. With all wisdom and insight he has made known to us the mystery of his will, according to his good pleasure that he set forth in Christ, as a plan for the fullness of time, to gather up all things in him, things in heaven and things on earth.

In Christ we have also obtained an inheritance, having been destined according to the purpose of him who accomplishes all things according to his counsel and will, so that we, who were the first to set our hope on Christ, might live for the praise of his glory.

In him you also, when you had heard the word of truth, the gospel of your salvation, and had believed in him, were marked with the seal of the promised Holy Spirit; this is the pledge of our inheritance toward redemption as God's own people, to the praise of his glory.

EPHESIANS 1:1-14, NRSV

INSIGHTS FROM WATCHMAN NEE

In the work of God today, things are often so constituted that we have no need to rely upon God. But the Lord's verdict upon all such work is uncompromising: "Apart from me ye can do nothing." Such work as man can do apart from God is wood, hay and stubble, and the test of fire will prove it so. For divine work can only be done with divine power, and that power is to be found in the Lord Jesus alone. It is made available to us in Him on the resurrection side of the cross. That is to say, it is when we have reached the point where, in all honesty, we cry: "I cannot speak," that we discover God is speaking. When we come to an end of our works, His work begins.

Thus, the fire in the days to come, and the cross today effect the same thing. What cannot stand the cross today will not survive the fire later. If my work, which is done in my power, is brought to death, how much comes out of the grave? Nothing! Nothing ever survives the cross but what is wholly of God in Christ.

God never asks us to do anything we can do. He asks us to live a life which we can never live and do a work that we can never do. Yet, by His grace, we are living it and doing it. The life we live is the life of Christ lived in the power of God, and the work we do is the work of Christ carried on through us by His Spirit whom we obey. Self is the only obstruction to that life and to that work. May we each one pray from our hearts: "O Lord, deal with me!"

Finally, the end and object of all work to which God can commit Himself must be His glory. This means that we get nothing out of it for ourselves. It is a divine principle that the less we get of personal gratification out of such a work, the greater is its true value to God. There is no room for glory to man in the work of God. True, there is a deep, precious joy in any service that brings Him pleasure and that opens the door to His working, but the ground of that joy is His glory and not man's. Everything is "to the praise of the glory of his grace" (see 1:6, 12, 14).

It is when these questions are truly settled between us and God that God will commit Himself—and indeed I believe He will allow us to say that then He has to do so. Experience in China has taught us this, that if there is ground for doubt whether our work is of God, then sure enough we find God is reluctant to answer prayer in relation to it. But when it is wholly of Him, He will commit Himself in wonderful ways. Then it is that, in utter obedience to Him, you can use His name, and all hell will have to recognize your authority to do so. When God commits Himself to a thing, then He comes out in power to prove that He is in it and is Himself its Author.

—*Sit, Walk, Stand*

QUESTIONS TO CONSIDER

1. How can you know if you are working in your power or God's power?
2. In what situation do you need to take authority through the name of Jesus?

A PRAYERFUL RESPONSE

Lord, teach me to work in Your power, for Your glory. Amen.

Whom Shall I Send?

THOUGHT FOR TODAY
God asks us to participate in the work of His kingdom.

WISDOM FROM SCRIPTURE
She was deeply distressed and prayed to the Lord, and wept bitterly.

She made this vow: "O Lord of hosts, if only you will look on the misery of your servant, and remember me, and not forget your servant, but will give to your servant a male child, then I will set him before you as a nazirite until the day of his death. He shall drink neither wine nor intoxicants, and no razor shall touch his head."

1 SAMUEL 1:10-11, NRSV

Then I heard the voice of the Lord saying, "Whom shall I send, and who will go for us?" And I said, "Here am I; send me!"

ISAIAH 6:8, NRSV

"Anyone who resolves to do the will of God will know whether the teaching is from God or whether I am speaking on my own."

JOHN 7:17, NRSV

We may clearly notice in the Bible that God needs man, since He needs his cooperation in order to accomplish His eternal plan. In the six days of creation, man is the center of God's work. After God has created man, He rests; for without man, He cannot rest. Although man afterwards falls, God's purpose concerning Him is not changed. He still wants to apprehend him. Man's salvation, man's edification, and man's spiritual maturity in life are all for the sake of satisfying God's need. In His work, God has a great need, which is, that He needs man's cooperation. It may be said that in God's work there is no place nor time when man does not participate. Man is called to work together with God; He must have man. (The work of God mentioned here does not, of course, include the six days of creative work, because the six days of creation were obviously undertaken by God alone, man having had no part in it.)

We may trace from Genesis to Revelation and see that God is always seeking, always apprehending, always leading and using man as the channel of His working. Before He does a thing, He first gets hold of man. And if He cannot obtain His man, He cannot do His work. Let us look at some illustrations of this fact.

The Lord Jesus always speaks about "the Son of Man" doing such and such, fully indicating that while He is on earth He always stands on the ground of the Son of Man. This is because God must accomplish His work through man. But, finding that man in general could not answer His demand, God sent His beloved Son to this world to be a man in order to answer His demand and accomplish His work. Some time afterward we see the Lord Jesus sending out the Twelve, and then the Seventy (Lk 9:1-2; 10:1). By this we can learn that for God to have His work done, He must always apprehend a people. From Genesis to Revelation we discover that all the works God has done among men are done by the hands of men. Without men, God cannot finish His work.

"Whom shall I send, and who will go for us?" asks God. The reason why many people are not being drawn into the kingdom is not because God has no desire to have the gospel preached, nor because He has no intention to save men, but because He does not have the man or men whom He can use. Many believers are possessed by vainglory; many Christians are engrossed in enjoyment; many are too occupied with their families; many are enslaved to comfort. These people care only for their own interests. They have no heart for preaching the gospel or doing God's work. Many people remain unsaved not because God has no will to save but because we do not cooperate with Him.

Oh! If every brother or sister were willing to cooperate with God, who could count the number of people He would save? The reason God's work is held back is because He does not have His man. Do let us realize that the Lord must have you and me before He can perform what He wants to do.

—*Whom Shall I Send?*

QUESTIONS TO CONSIDER

1. Are you willing to cooperate with God's call to service?
2. What will this mean in your daily life?

A PRAYERFUL RESPONSE

Lord, I will accept Your call to me for service. Amen.

The Way of Consecration

THOUGHT FOR TODAY

Whatever our employment, God calls us into His service.

WISDOM FROM SCRIPTURE

Oh, the depth of the riches of the wisdom and knowledge of God! How unsearchable his judgments, and his paths beyond tracing out!

"Who has known the mind of the Lord? Or who has been his counselor?"

"Who has ever given to God, that God should repay him?"

For from him and through him and to him are all things. To him be the glory forever! Amen.

Therefore, I urge you, brothers, in view of God's mercy, to offer your bodies as living sacrifices, holy and pleasing to God—this is your spiritual act of worship.

Do not conform any longer to the pattern of this world, but be transformed by the renewing of your mind. Then you will be able to test and approve what God's will is—his good, pleasing and perfect will.

For by the grace given me I say to every one of you: Do not think of yourself more highly than you ought, but rather think of yourself with sober judgment, in accordance with the measure of faith God has given you.

Just as each of us has one body with many members, and these members do not all have the same function, so in Christ we who are many form one body, and each member belongs to all the others.

ROMANS 11:33–12:5, NIV

Consecration aims not at preaching or working for God, but in serving God. The word *service* in the original bears the sense of "waiting on," that is, waiting on God in order to serve Him. Consecration does not necessarily involve incessant labor, for its aim is to wait upon God. If He wishes us to stand, we stand; if He wants us to wait, we wait; if He desires us to run, we run. This is the true meaning of "waiting on" Him.

What God requires of us is to present our bodies to Him, not for the purpose of ascending the pulpit or of evangelizing far distant lands, but of waiting upon Him. Some may indeed have to accept the pulpit, because they are sent there by God. Some may be constrained to go to distant lands, for they are commissioned by God to go. The work itself varies but the time consumed remains the same—our lifetime. We need to learn to wait on God. We offer our bodies that we may be those who serve.

Once we become Christians, we must serve God for life. As soon as a medical doctor becomes a Christian, medicine recedes from being his vocation to his avocation. So will it be for the engineer. The Lord's demand occupies the first priority; serving God becomes the major job. Should the Lord permit, the doctor and engineer can do some medical or engineering work to maintain a living, but they will not be able to make either of them their life's work. Some of the early disciples were fishermen, but after they followed the Lord, they did not hope any more to be great and successful fishermen. They might be allowed to fish occasionally, but their destiny was altered.

May God be gracious to us, especially to young believers, that we may all see how our vocation has been changed. Let all the professors, doctors, nurses, engineers and industrialists see that their vocation is now to serve God. Their past vocations have receded to avocations. They should not be too ambitious in their special fields, though the Lord may still give some of them special positions. We who serve God cannot expect to be prosperous in the world, for these two are contradictory. Hereafter, we are to serve God alone; we have no other way or destiny.

In consecration, our prayer is: "O Lord, You have given me the opportunity and privilege to come before You and serve You. Lord, I am Yours. Henceforth my ears, hands and feet, being bought by the blood, are exclusively Yours. The world can no longer use them, nor will I use them either." What, then, is the result? The result will be holiness, for the fruit of consecration is holiness. In Exodus 28 we have consecration on the one hand and holiness to the Lord on the other.

We need to be brought to see that after we become Christians, we are spoiled for everything else. This does not mean we will be less faithful in our secular jobs. No, we must be subject to authorities and faithfully fulfill our tasks. But we have seen before God that our life must be spent in the way of serving God; all other jobs are sidelines.

There is a chorus which runs: "I am His, I am His. Glory to His name, for I am His." Though the refrain is simple, it must have been written by one who knew what consecration is. Such a song can only be sung by redeemed ones. And only redeemed ones can consecrate themselves.

I feel strongly during these years that the way consecration is preached is wrong. It should not be preached as if we were begging people to consecrate; we should tell people instead that the way is now open for consecration. If I hang out a placard, announcing that I am commissioned to find those with ability to work for the president, I suppose many will invite me for dinner; many will seek for the job of serving the president. Is it not strange that we beg people to come to serve God? Let me tell you, there is a way open for you to serve the Lord of Hosts. You come to serve God, not to do God a favor.

Perhaps, though, I desire to serve God but am uncertain as to whether I will be accepted. The Old Testament passages show us that we do have God's permission to consecrate ourselves. The New Testament confirms this by saying that by the compassion of God I should present myself to Him, for it is my spiritual service. To be privileged to be God's slaves is our greatest honor.

—*A Living Sacrifice*

QUESTIONS TO CONSIDER

1. Have you presented your whole life to God?
2. How has God called you to serve Him through your daily work, whether inside or outside the home?

A PRAYERFUL RESPONSE

Lord, as my reasonable service, I give You my entire life. Amen.

The Foundation of Ministry

THOUGHT FOR TODAY

To minister, we need fresh revelations from God.

WISDOM FROM SCRIPTURE

"Beware of false prophets, who come to you in sheep's clothing but inwardly are ravenous wolves.

"You will know them by their fruits. Are grapes gathered from thorns, or figs from thistles?

"In the same way, every good tree bears good fruit, but the bad tree bears bad fruit.

"A good tree cannot bear bad fruit, nor can a bad tree bear good fruit.

"Every tree that does not bear good fruit is cut down and thrown into the fire.

"Thus you will know them by their fruits.

"Not everyone who says to me, 'Lord, Lord,' will enter the kingdom of heaven, but only the one who does the will of my Father in heaven.

"On that day many will say to me, 'Lord, Lord, did we not prophesy in your name, and cast out demons in your name, and do many deeds of power in your name?'

"Then I will declare to them, 'I never knew you; go away from me, you evil-doers.'"

MATTHEW 7:15-23, NRSV

When we touch the subject of ministry we should understand that there are two kinds of revelation; the basic, which is given once for all, and the detailed, which is given time and again. When you receive the revelation of Christ, you obtain the basic revelation, the same which Paul once received. Later on, you discover from the Bible that what you have already seen before the Lord is this basic revelation. In seeing the Lord, your total being has fallen down before God. You know that nothing you once possessed can now stand, not even your zealousness in serving God—much as Paul had once done.

Let us realize that Saul of Tarsus was felled to the ground. This prostration of his was not that of sin, but of work; not of coldness, but of zeal. He knew the law, he was familiar with the Old Testament, he was more zealous than his contemporary Pharisees. He was so full of zeal that he laid aside everything to persecute the church. He felt that this was serving God, and he served in an absolute way. Setting aside his error for the moment, it must be admitted that his zeal was very real. Yet he instantly fell down when struck by light. He quickly saw that his past had been spent in persecuting the Lord, not in serving Him at all.

Many may be saved and yet still be blind in this matter of service or work, even as Saul was blind. Saul thought he was in the way of serving God, yet when he was enlightened by the Lord he cried out from the depth of his being, "What shall I do, Lord?" Perhaps this is a question many have never encountered. They have never been moved by the Holy Spirit to address the Lord as Lord. They may only be calling "Lord, Lord," just as those in Matthew 7, but never have called Jesus as Lord, according to 1 Corinthians 12. Here in Saul we see one who confessed for the first time Jesus of Nazareth as Lord and who also asked for the first time, "What shall I do, Lord?" He had fallen down—down from his work, his zeal, his righteousness. Upon experiencing this fundamental seeing, the Bible became a new book—an opened book—to him.

Many people depend on instructions or references in studying the Bible; they do not know the Scriptures through meeting the Lord. But how marvelous: as soon as anyone meets the Lord and receives enlightenment, the Bible becomes a new book to him. One brother, speaking out of his experience, once said, "When the Lord puts me under His light, what I get that day is enough for me to speak for a month." First you must have this basic revelation; and out of that, many more revelations will be given to you. When you have received this fundamental revelation you will discover God speaking here and there throughout the Scriptures. Day after day you will receive many fragmentary revelations which you can use in serving people. This is called ministry.

Ministry, therefore, is based upon our getting a word before God. We have met Christ, and we want to serve the church with the Christ we know; and for this we need to have revelation each time we serve. Ministry requires our seeing something before God and in freshness presenting this thing to the church. Revelations, we have said, are of two kinds: the basic and the detailed, the "once for all" and "the time and again." Without possessing the first it is impossible to have the second. Only after you have secured the basic is your spirit usable; only then is your knowledge of the Lord and that of the Bible usable, and only then are you usable.

Even so, you still cannot simply go out and minister. It is true that this basic revelation makes you a minister, but when you do minister you need detailed revelations added to the foundational one. Ministry is founded on the basic understanding and revelation, but when God sends you out to speak today, you must learn how to receive the particular revelation for that day, before God. Not because I have once received revelation am I therefore able to speak. Each time I minister I need to receive special revelation for the occasion. Each revelation brings in service, each revelation gives a special supply, each revelation constitutes a ministry.

The basic revelation once given will not supply enough for a lifetime; it only serves as the basis for a fuller and continuous revelation before God. The first revelation brings in many more revelations. Without the first there can be no additional; but with the first, many more will be given. Not because a person has once received the basic revelation can he thereafter minister with that revelation for years, or for a lifetime. If we need to depend momentarily on the Lord for our life, we in like measure need to do so for our work. Each revelation we receive gives birth to each new ministry. It requires many revelations for many times of ministry. Let us keep in mind that each revelation is only sufficient for one occasion of ministry, not for two. Nevertheless, all these detailed revelations are based on the fundamental one.

These foundational problems must be solved before there is the possibility of our being ministers of God's word. Revelation after revelation must continuously be added; no one revelation can supply unlimited ministry. Each revelation affords ministry for one occasion; each gives one service. It never means having several sermons prepared in advance, which we can use whenever an occasion arises. It cannot be that I have one sermon memorized on which I can speak at any time. We should understand that we speak God's word, not ours. You may have memorized a speech by heart, yet if you are going to minister God's word, you need to have Him speak to you first. Continuous revelation begets continual ministry.

—*The Ministry of God's Word*

QUESTIONS TO CONSIDER

1. How can you seek God for His word to you?
2. What might keep you from "continuous revelation" and "continual ministry"?

A PRAYERFUL RESPONSE

Lord, as I minister to others, I want to speak Your words, not mine. Amen.

Lights in the World

THOUGHT FOR TODAY

We are to be salt and light in the world.

WISDOM FROM SCRIPTURE

[Jesus said,] "You are the salt of the earth; but if salt has lost its taste, how can its saltiness be restored? It is no longer good for anything, but is thrown out and trampled under foot.

"You are the light of the world. A city built on a hill cannot be hid.

"No one after lighting a lamp puts it under the bushel basket, but on the lamp-stand, and it gives light to all in the house.

"In the same way, let your light shine before others, so that they may see your good works and give glory to your Father in heaven.

"Do not think that I have come to abolish the law or the prophets; I have come not to abolish but to fulfill.

"For truly I tell you, until heaven and earth pass away, not one letter, not one stroke of a letter, will pass from the law until all is accomplished.

"Therefore, whoever breaks one of the least of these commandments, and teaches others to do the same, will be called least in the kingdom of heaven; but whoever does them and teaches them will be called great in the kingdom of heaven.

"For I tell you, unless your righteousness exceeds that of the scribes and Pharisees, you will never enter the kingdom of heaven."

—MATTHEW 5:13-20, NRSV

Far from seeking to avoid the world, we need to see how privileged we are to have been placed there by God. "As thou hast sent me into the world, even so have I also sent them into the world" (Jn 19:18). What a statement! The Church is Jesus' successor, a divine settlement planted here right in the midst of Satan's territory. It is something that Satan cannot abide, any more than he could abide Jesus Himself, and yet it is something that he cannot by any means rid himself of. It is a colony of heaven, an alien intrusion on his territory, and one against which he is utterly powerless.

"Children of God," Paul calls us, "in the midst of a crooked and perverse generation, among whom ye are seen as lights in the world" (Phil 2:15). God has deliberately placed us in the cosmos to show it up for what it is. We are to expose it to the divine light, for all men to see its God-defying rebelliousness on the one hand, and its hollowness and emptiness on the other.

And our task does not stop there. We are to proclaim to men the good news that if they will turn to it that light of God in the face of Jesus Christ will set them free from the world's vain emptiness, into the fullness that is His. It is this twofold mission of the Church that accounts for Satan's hatred. There is nothing that goads him so much as the Church's presence in the world. Nothing would please him more than to see its telltale light removed. The Church is a thorn in the side of God's adversary, a constant source of irritation and annoyance to him. We make a heap of trouble for Satan, simply by being in the world. So why leave it?

"Go ye into all the world and preach the gospel" (Mk

16:15). This is the Christian's privilege. It is also his duty. Those who try to opt out of the world only demonstrate that they are still, in some degree, in bondage to its ways of thinking. We who are "not of it" have no reason at all to try to leave it, for it is where we should be.

So there is no need for us to give up our secular employments. Far from it, for they are our mission field. In this matter there are no secular considerations, only spiritual ones. We do not live our lives in separate compartments, as Christians in the Church and as secular beings the rest of the time. There is not a thing in our profession or in our employment that God intends should be dissociated from our life as His children. Everything we do, be it in field or highway, in shop, factory, kitchen, hospital or school, has spiritual value in terms of the kingdom of Christ. Everything is to be claimed for Him.

Satan would much prefer to have no Christians in any of these places, for they are decidedly in his way there. He tries therefore to frighten us out of the world, and if he cannot do that, to get us involved in his world system, thinking in its terms, regulating our behavior by its standards. Either would be a triumph for him. But for us to be in the world, yet with all our hopes, all our interests, and all our prospects out of the world, that is Satan's defeat and God's glory.

Of Jesus' presence in the world it is written that "the darkness overcame it not" (Jn 1:5). Nowhere in Scripture does it tell us of sin that we are to "overcome" it, but it distinctly says we are to overcome the world. In relation to sin, God's Word speaks only of deliverance; it is in relation to the world that it speaks of victory.

We need deliverance from sin because God never intended that we should have any touch with it; but we do not need, nor should we seek, deliverance from the world, for it is in the purpose of God that we touch it. We are not delivered out of the world, but being born from above, we have victory over it, and we have that victory in the same sense, and with the same unfailing certainty, that light overcame darkness.

—*Love Not the World*

QUESTIONS TO CONSIDER

1. In what mission field has God placed you?
2. How can you reflect Christ there?

A PRAYERFUL RESPONSE

Lord, with You I will defeat darkness in this world. Amen.

An Unashamed Worker

THOUGHT FOR TODAY

God values our inward purity more than outward success.

WISDOM FROM SCRIPTURE

Do your best to present yourself to God as one approved by him, a worker who has no need to be ashamed, rightly explaining the word of truth.

Avoid profane chatter, for it will lead people into more and more impiety, and their talk will spread like gangrene. Among them are Hymenaeus and Philetus, who have swerved from the truth by claiming that the resurrection has already taken place. They are upsetting the faith of some.

But God's firm foundation stands, bearing this inscription; "The Lord knows those who are his" and "Let everyone who calls on the name of the Lord turn away from wickedness."

In a large house there are utensils not only of gold and silver but also of wood and clay, some for special use, some for ordinary.

All who cleanse themselves of the things I have mentioned will become special utensils, dedicated and useful to the owner of the house, ready for every good work.

Shun youthful passions and pursue righteousness, faith, love, and peace, along with those who call on the Lord from a pure heart.

Have nothing to do with stupid and senseless controversies; you know that they breed quarrels.

And the Lord's servant must not be quarrelsome but kindly to everyone, an apt teacher, patient, correcting opponents with gentleness. God may perhaps grant that they will repent and come to know the truth, and that they may escape from the snare of the devil, having been held captive by him to do his will.

2 TIMOTHY 2:15-26, NRSV

INSIGHTS FROM WATCHMAN NEE

We do not work for work's sake, we work according to the will of God. We cannot live in the work; rather, we must live in the life of Christ.

The foundation of our work is life, and the way of the work is the cross. Unless a thing is done in life and has undergone the dealings of the cross, it cannot be reckoned as work. Hence, it behooves us not to stress the outer work more than the inner life of Christ. Real service, providing true supply, must be done in life.

God pays attention to the person more than anything else. If the person is not right, none of his works will be right. To an unreliable man, the word *work* is not even in his vocabulary. But to the right man, there is no fear of having no work to do.

For this reason we do not cast out demons merely for the sake of casting out demons, nor do we preach the gospel simply for the sake of preaching the gospel. Everything done is for God's sake. When God moves us, we move. When He is still, we keep still. We cannot depart from God and be active in external work.

One whose life is rich and strong has no fear of not working. The greater one's ministry is, the wider his service will be.

For service is based on a person's ministry.

I once saw a doctor who kept very busy, even after his retirement. Many still went to consult him. Where there is sugar, there will be ants who need no special invitation.

Before we can talk about work, we must first be touched and broken by the Lord, and be brought by Him to a right condition.

We must first receive grace. May there be a beginning in our lives, when whatever is of the flesh and of man, be it opinion, method or idea, is cast aside.

The problem today lies not in teaching, for teaching cannot solve any difficulty. What is required is practical learning and exercise, the dealing with self in many areas of failure.

Hence, we need to be more humble, more yielding and more dying to self. We must not live in ourselves, but instead allow God to live in us.

The cross is absolutely essential, because without death there can be no life. The measure of life is based on the degree of death. The apostle Paul observed this: "always bearing about in the body the dying of the Lord Jesus, that the life also of Jesus might be made manifest in our body. For we who live are always delivered unto death for Jesus' sake, that the life also of Jesus might be made manifest in our mortal flesh. So then death worketh in us, but life in you" (2 Cor 4:10-12).

He who rejects the cross is never able to live out life. One must be broken, since brokenness is the way of the release of the spirit. The breaking of the man and the releasing of the spirit is a most fundamental lesson.

The heart of the matter is therefore man. The principal dealing to emphasize is to make man right. Some people do not experience much change, whereas others show great change. The reason is because some have not really gotten hold of the spiritual reality, whereas others grasp hold of the real thing.

It is of prime importance that the man be right. He must receive grace and be brought into a right condition.

—*Gleanings in the Fields of Boaz*

QUESTIONS TO CONSIDER

1. Are you in right standing with God?
2. How can you learn to value inner purity more than outward success?

A PRAYERFUL RESPONSE

Lord, I want to be in right standing before You. Amen.

Be Diligent

THOUGHT FOR TODAY
Diligence characterizes God's servants.

WISDOM FROM SCRIPTURE
[Jesus said,] "But the one who had received the one talent went off and dug a hole in the ground and hid his master's money.

"After a long time the master of those slaves came and settled accounts with them.

"Then the one who had received the five talents came forward, bringing five more talents, saying, 'Master, you handed over to me five talents; see, I have made five more talents.'

"His master said to him, 'Well done, good and trustworthy slave; you have been trustworthy in a few things, I will put you in charge of many things; enter into the joy of your master.'

"And the one with the two talents also came forward, saying, 'Master, you handed over to me two talents; see, I have made two more talents.'

"His master said to him, 'Well done, good and trustworthy slave; you have been trustworthy in a few things, I will put you in charge of many things; enter into the joy of your master.'

"Then the one who had received the one talent also came forward, saying, 'Master, I knew that you were a harsh man, reaping where you did not sow, and gathering where you did not scatter seed; so I was afraid, and I went and hid your talent in the ground. Here you have what is yours.'

"But his master replied, 'You wicked and lazy slave! You knew, did you, that I reap where I did not sow, and gather where I did not scatter?

"'Then you ought to have invested my money with the bankers, and on my return I would have received what was my own with interest.

"'So I take the talent from him, and give it to the one with ten talents.

"'For to all those who have, more will be given, and they will have an abundance; but from those who have nothing, even what they have will be taken away.

"'As for this worthless slave, throw him into the outer darkness, where there will be weeping and gnashing of teeth.'"

MATTHEW 25:18-30, NRSV

INSIGHTS FROM WATCHMAN NEE

This passage of Scripture shows us that diligence is also a basic requirement of the Lord's workman. Our Lord Jesus plainly points out to us the two fundamental flaws in the character of this servant: one, that he is "wicked," and the other, that he is "slothful." He is wicked because he accuses his lord of being a hard man, reaping where he has not sowed and gathering where he has not scattered.

The other flaw about this servant is that he is slothful. When he buries the talent in the earth, what his heart meditates is "wicked," but what his hand does is "slothful." He imagines in his heart the kind of master his lord is. His thought is evil in content. And in burying the talent in the earth, he does not do what he ought to do. Such action reveals none other trait than that of slothfulness. Let us acknowledge here that laziness constitutes the major problem for many people.

A lazy person will not seek out work to do. Even when he definitely sees work, he still hopes there is none! Many Christians seem to adopt this same attitude, wherein a big thing dissolves into a small thing, and a small thing dissolves into no thing—that is to say, nothing; wherein a large work fades into a little work, and a little work disappears into no work. According to experience, there is but one kind of person useful in the work of God, and that is the diligent person. Lazy people are most despicable. One brother has said that even Satan deems the slothful to be useless.

"A slothful man hideth his hand in his dish, and will not so much as bring it to his mouth again" (Prv 19:24). A person who is slothful is unwilling to do anything. Why? Because he is afraid of getting tired, even in the matter of feeding himself! His hand is in the dish all right, yet he is too lazy even to bring it back to his mouth with food in it. He must eat, but he even expects someone else to bring the food to his mouth! Without any doubt, there is one class of people in the world who are utterly useless—they are the lazy and slothful. God never uses such a person.

Let me ask you, have you ever seen a lazy person serving God well? All who are used of the Lord labor hard in His service. They do not waste their time or their energy. Those who daily and constantly only anticipate rest for themselves do not look like God's servants at all. For His servants do not know how to live indolently; they are always about the business of redeeming their time.

—*The Character of God's Workman*

QUESTIONS TO CONSIDER

1. In what areas of life could you be more diligent?
2. What barriers keep you from making these changes?

A PRAYERFUL RESPONSE

Lord, make me a more diligent servant. Amen.

Service in the Body of Christ

THOUGHT FOR TODAY

Members of the body of Christ belong to and support one another.

WISDOM FROM SCRIPTURE

For as in one body we have many members, and not all the members have the same function, so we, who are many, are one body in Christ, and individually we are members one of another.

We have gifts that differ according to the grace given to us: prophecy, in proportion to faith; ministry, in ministering; the teacher, in teaching; the exhorter, in exhortation; the giver, in generosity; the leader, in diligence; the compassionate, in cheerfulness.

ROMANS 12:4-8, NRSV

INSIGHTS FROM WATCHMAN NEE

How many of us who are Christians know that we are not only believers but also members of the body of Christ? We ought to understand that in the Adamic life there is not just the sinful or the natural that needs to be dealt with; the individualistic character must also be dealt with.

What do I mean by the individualistic character in the Adamic life? It is that attitude of life which insists on maintaining my independent existence, my independent living, or my individual action as though I were the only one living in the world. This kind of life hinders a person from entering into the reality of the body of Christ. We should know that the antithesis of the body is the individual. For us to enter into the reality of the body, we must be delivered from individualism.

The body of Christ is not just a teaching. The body of Christ needs to be entered into experientially. Whoever has not entered in does not know what is within. He who is saved can easily detect another who is saved; in like manner, the one who has already entered into the reality of the body of Christ may also discern quickly whether others have entered into the reality of it or not. When you are saved you have not only heard the doctrine of salvation but also have seen that Christ is the living life. In salvation you enter a new realm, and clearly see the situation of the unsaved in retrospect.

Similarly, those who truly live in the body of Christ may vividly perceive the conditions of all who have not lived in the body. People may understand the book of Romans and not be saved; likewise, men may appreciate the letter of Ephesians and not know the body of Christ. When you forsake sin and enter into Christ, you are saved. But you need to be delivered from being individualistic in order to enter experientially into the body of Christ.

God permits us to be individuals, but He does not allow us to be individualistic. Before we enter experientially into the body of Christ, we are full of individualism. Even our spiritual pursuit is inspired by this trait. Why seek for holiness? That I myself may be holy. Why desire for power? That I personally may have power. Why look for fruits of labor? That I individually may have fruits. Why wish for the kingdom? That I myself may possess the kingdom. Everything is bound up with "I." This is not the body; this is individualism.

Just as Peter, at Pentecost, preached, and three thousand people were saved in one day, so I dream of saving three thousand in one day that I too may produce many fruits. Yet we need to recall that the eleven other apostles stood up with Peter. Did the other apostles ever jealously complain, saying that if Peter could save many people, they too should be able to do the same? Or did Peter ever build up in his mind a high tower of boasting, saying that he could save people whom others could not? We know that no such thing ever happened. For God does not look for an individual vessel but is out to get a corporate one. If you truly see the body of Christ, you will neither be jealous nor proud. Whether the work is done by you or by me or by others makes no difference. All of this is a body matter, nothing is purely individual.

We therefore need to see ourselves not only as believers but even more so as a member. I am a member; hence I am not the whole—not even the half—but only a small part of Christ's body. It is unquestionably a tremendous deliverance to see the body and to recognize oneself as only a member. Formerly many things were centered on our individual selves. Whether it was work or living, all was highly individualistic. One day, when we discerned the body, we were naturally delivered from individualism.

In salvation we first see Christ and then we are saved. By the same token, we first see the body and then quite naturally we are delivered from individualism, and become members of the body in reality. Not in the sense that we outwardly say we will act according to the principles of the body when we are faced with a situation, but in the sense of acting according to the principle of the body because we have received the revelation and have entered experientially into the body of Christ. With the natural life being dealt with, we spontaneously perceive that we are members.

—*The Body of Christ: A Reality*

QUESTIONS TO CONSIDER

1. Do you see yourself as an individual in the body, or individualistic? Why?
2. What gifts have you been given with which to serve the body?

A PRAYERFUL RESPONSE

Lord, thank You that I am not alone, but am part of Your body. Amen.

Becoming Overcomers

THOUGHT FOR TODAY

God often uses a few to reach the many.

WISDOM FROM SCRIPTURE

"Let anyone who has an ear listen to what the Spirit is saying to the churches. To everyone who conquers, I will give permission to eat from the tree of life that is in the paradise of God.

"Let anyone who has an ear listen to what the Spirit is saying to the churches. Whoever conquers will not be harmed by the second death.

"Let anyone who has an ear listen to what the Spirit is saying to the churches. To everyone who conquers I will give some of the hidden manna, and I will give a white stone, and on the white stone is written a new name that no one knows except the one who receives it.

"To everyone who conquers and continues to do my works to the end, I will give authority over the nations;

"If you conquer, you will be clothed like them in white robes, and I will not blot your name out of the book of life; I will confess your name before my Father and before his angels.

"If you conquer, I will make you a pillar in the temple of my God; you will never go out of it. I will write on you the name of my God, and the name of the city of my God, the new Jerusalem that comes down from my God out of heaven, and my own new name.

"To the one who conquers I will give a place with me on my throne, just as I myself conquered and sat down with my Father on his throne."

REVELATION 2:7, 11, 17, 26; 3:5, 12, 21, NRSV

INSIGHTS FROM WATCHMAN NEE

Now whenever the church fails, God finds a few in the church—called to be overcomers—that they might bear the responsibility which the church as a whole ought to, but fails to bear. He chooses a company of the faithful few to represent the church in the demonstration of the victory of Christ. He has His overcomers in all the seven periods of the church (as represented by the seven churches described in Revelation chapters 2 and 3). This overcomer line is never cut. The overcomers are not some special class. They are simply a group of people who conform to the original plan of God.

The way God works, as illustrated in His Holy Scriptures, is to find a few as a nucleus in order to reach the many. This was true in the patriarchal age. At that time God chose people individually: those such as Abel, Enoch, Noah and Abraham. Later on, through Abraham (the few), God reaches the whole nation of Israel (the many)—that is to say, God reaches the dispensation of the law through the patriarchal age. Then from the dispensation of the law (the nation of Israel), God reaches to the dispensation of grace (the church out of all nations); and likewise from the dispensation of grace, He will reach to the dispensation of the kingdom (the entire world); and from the dispensation of the kingdom, to the new heaven and the new earth (the new creation), for the kingdom is the prologue to the new heaven and the new earth. So then, the principle of God's operation is from the few to the many.

The Head, from whom all the body by joints and bands having nourishment ministered and knit together, increaseth with the increase of God" (Col 2:19). The joints are for supplying, while the bands are for knitting. The Head holds the body together through these joints and bands. And these joints and bands are overcomers.

Jerusalem typifies the whole church, whereas Zion—which is in Jerusalem—represents the overcomers in the church. Jerusalem is larger than Zion, yet Zion is the stronghold of Jerusalem. What answers to the heart of God is called Zion; that which speaks of the failure and sins of the Jews is called Jerusalem. God allows Jerusalem to be trodden down, but He usually keeps Zion intact. There will be a new Jerusalem, but there is no new Zion, because Zion never grows old.

Each time the relationship between Zion and Jerusalem is mentioned in the Old Testament, we are shown that the characteristics, life, blessing and establishing of Jerusalem are invariably derived from Zion. The elders were in Jerusalem, the ark was to be in Zion (see 1 Kgs 8:1). God does good in His good pleasure to Zion, and He builds the walls of Jerusalem (see Ps 51:18). God's name is in Zion, while His praise is in Jerusalem (see Ps 102:21). God blesses out of Zion, and Jerusalem receives the good of it (see Ps 128:5). The Lord dwells in Jerusalem, yet He receives praises out of Zion (see Ps 135:21). God speaks first to Zion, and then the good tidings reach Jerusalem (see Is 41:27). He dwells in Zion and thus sanctifies Jerusalem (see Jl 3:17).

God today is seeking, among the defeated church, 144,000 (a representative figure, to be sure) to stand on mount Zion (see Rev 14:1). Each and every time, He uses relatively few believers as channels to pour forth life into the church for her revival. As their Lord did, these few must pour forth blood in order to let life flow. The overcomers are to stand on the ground of victory for the church, and instead of the church. They are to endure sufferings and shames.

Therefore, God's overcomers must forsake all self-complacencies, pay the cost, let the cross cut off all that comes out of the old creation, and stand against the gates of Hades (see Mt 16:18).

Are you willing to hurt your own heart that you may gain God's heart? Are you ready to let yourself be defeated so that the Lord may triumph? When your obedience is made full, God will quickly avenge all the disobedience (see 2 Cor 10:6).

—God's Plan and the Overcomers

QUESTIONS TO CONSIDER
1. In the past, how have you been an overcomer?
2. In what area is God asking you to now overcome?

A PRAYERFUL RESPONSE
Lord, I know that with You all things are possible. Amen.

Run the Race

THOUGHT FOR TODAY

We can joyfully run the race before us.

WISDOM FROM SCRIPTURE

Therefore, since we are surrounded by so great a cloud of witnesses, let us also lay aside every weight and the sin that clings so closely, and let us run with perseverance the race that is set before us, looking to Jesus the pioneer and perfecter of our faith, who for the sake of the joy that was set before him endured the cross, disregarding its shame and has taken his seat at the right hand of the throne of God.

Consider him who endured such hostility against himself from sinners, so that you may not grow weary or lose heart.

In your struggle against sin you have not yet resisted to the point of shedding your blood.

And you have forgotten the exhortation that addresses you as children—

"My child, do not regard lightly the discipline of the Lord, or lose heart when you are punished by him;

for the Lord disciplines those whom he loves, and chastises every child whom he accepts."

Endure trials for the sake of discipline, God is treating you as children; for what child is there whom a parent does not discipline?

If you do not have that discipline in which all children share, then you are illegitimate and not his children.

Moreover, we had human parents to discipline us, and we respected them. Should we not be even more willing to be subject to the Father of spirits and live?

For they disciplined us for a short time as seemed best to them, but he disciplines us for our good, in order that we may share his holiness.

Now, discipline always seems painful rather than pleasant at the time, but later it yields the peaceful fruit of righteousness to those who have been trained by it.

Therefore lift your drooping hands and strengthen your weak knees, and make straight paths for your feet, so that what is lame may not be put out of joint, but rather be healed.

Pursue peace with everyone, and the holiness without which no one will see the Lord.

HEBREWS 12:1-14, NRSV

INSIGHTS FROM WATCHMAN NEE

God places two considerations before men: first, He presents eternal life to sinners; and second, He presents the kingdom to all who already have eternal life. All who believe have eternal life; nevertheless, as Jesus said to His believing disciples, "Except your righteousness shall exceed the righteousness of the scribes and Pharisees, ye shall in no wise enter into the kingdom of heaven" (Mt 5:20). The Lord Jesus also declared this: "Not every one that saith unto me, Lord, Lord, shall enter into the kingdom of heaven; but he that doeth the will of my Father who is in heaven" (Mt 7:21). Thus we are shown that to have eternal life one need only believe, but to enter the kingdom one is required to fulfill another condition.

Soon after a person is saved he is set by God on a specific

course that lies ahead of him. The entire life of a Christian can be likened to running a race. Yet this is not a racing toward the goal of eternal life. It does not mean that he who wins this race will have as his prize eternal life; on the contrary, only the person who has eternal life is qualified to run. No, the result of this race is that some of the participants are to be crowned while others will not be (see 1 Cor 9:24-25).

What is meant by the crown? The crown represents the kingdom. It signifies reigning, having dominion and glory. And thus to obtain the crown means to gain the kingdom— that is to say, to reign with the Lord Jesus and to have dominion and glory. And to lose the crown means to not have the kingdom—a not reigning with the Lord nor receiving dominion and glory. Hence the crown is the symbol of the kingdom. For a Christian, having eternal life is already a settled matter, but having the kingdom depends on how that Christian runs.

As soon as a person is saved he is set by God on a course which leads to the kingdom. His words, his conduct, his thoughts, his life—in fact, his everything—is related to whether or not he may gain the kingdom. Now the believer who refuses to run the race judges himself as being unfit for the kingdom; and the believer who runs poorly jeopardizes his chances of winning the kingdom. Now God has already placed every Christian on this course. Yet whether or not he shall win the kingdom is a matter that can only be decided by his own self. His consecration, faithfulness and victory will help him to receive the crown. But for those who love the world and follow after the flesh, they shall not gain the kingdom of heaven—even though they are the possessors of eternal life by having trusted in the Lord Jesus.

—*The Testimony of God*

QUESTIONS TO CONSIDER
1. Is it your desire to run the race God has set before you?
2. How does the "joy set before you" encourage you to keep running?

A PRAYERFUL RESPONSE
Lord, help me to run with perseverance the race set before me. Amen.

BOOKS BY WATCHMAN NEE

A Balanced Christian Life

A Living Sacrifice

Aids to "Revelation"

Assembling Together

Back to the Cross

"Come, Lord Jesus"

Do All to the Glory of God

From Faith to Faith

From Glory to Glory

Full of Grace and Truth

Gleanings in the Fields of
   Boaz

God's Plan and the
   Overcomers

Gospel Dialogue

Grace for Grace

Interpreting Matthew

Let Us Pray

Love Not the World

Love One Another

Not I But Christ

Practical Issues of This Life

Sit, Walk, Stand

Spiritual Authority

Spiritual Reality or Obsession

Song of Songs

Take Heed

The Better Covenant

The Body of Christ: A Reality

The Character of God's
   Workman

The Finest of the Wheat,
   Volume 1

The Finest of the Wheat,
   Volume 2

The Glory of His Life

The Good Confession

The Joyful Heart

The King and the Kingdom
   of Heaven

The Latent Power of the Soul

The Lord, My Portion

The Messenger of the Cross

The Ministry of God's Word

The Mystery of Creation

The Normal Christian Life

The Release of the Spirit

The Salvation of the Soul

The Spirit of the Gospel

The Spirit of Judgment

The Spirit of Wisdom and
   Revelation

The Testimony of God

What Shall This Man Do?

Whom Shall I Send?

Ye Search the Scriptures

ABOUT THE COMPILER

With the *Life Messages* devotional series, Judith Couchman hopes you'll be encouraged and enlightened by people who have shared their spiritual journeys through the printed word.

Judith owns Judith & Company, a writing and editing business. She has also served as the creator and founding editor-in-chief of *Clarity* magazine, managing editor of *Christian Life,* editor of *Sunday Digest,* director of communications for The Navigators, and director of new product development for NavPress.

Besides speaking to women's and professional groups, Judith is the author-compiler of thirty-five books and many magazine articles. In addition, she has received numerous awards for her work in secondary education, religious publishing, and corporate communications.

She lives in Colorado.